ATE DUE

Nancy Polette's How-To Book of Literature-Based Reading

The Whole Language Feast

HOLISTIC

IMMERSION

READING ALOUD

LITERATURE BASED

READING FOR MEANING

STRATEGIES

WRITING PROCESS

LANGUAGE EXPERIENCE

COLLABORATIVE

FLEXIBLE GROUPING

THEMATIC STUDIES

INTEGRATED

CHILD CENTERED

Copyright © 1991 by Nancy Polette

P. O. Box 0455
O'Fallon, MO 63366

ISBN 0-913839-88-4

Printed in U. S. A.

Book Lures Inc.

TABLE OF CONTENTS

TABLE OF CONTENTS (continued)

THE WHOLE LANGUAGE FEAST

You don't have to eat every bite to enjoy the meal!

HOLISTIC

IMMERSION

READING

ALOUD

LITERATURE BASED

READING FOR MEANING

STRATEGIES

WRITING PROCESS

LANGUAGE EXPERIENCE

COLLABORATIVE

FLEXIBLE GROUPING

THEMATIC STUDIES

INTEGRATED

CHILD CENTERED

© 1990 N. Polette

PRE-READING ACTIVITY!

Before reading the definition of WHOLE LANGUAGE on the next page, group these terms under the correct headings. Support or deny your groupings by reading the definition on page three.

1. teacher as a leader
2. language across the curriculum
3. processes to be learned
4. basal reader
5. technicians
6. teacher as a facilitator
7. science of teaching
8. labeling
9. any meaningful print
10. separate subjects
11. philosophy
12. products to be tested
13. flexible grouping
14. ability grouping

Group the above terms under these two categories

Traditional Program	Whole Language Program

WHOLE LANGUAGE IS ...

Many teachers across the U. S. have been moving toward Whole Language instruction in their classroom during the past few years.

Whole Language is not a method of teaching reading or any particular program or set of materials. It is a philosophy or way of thinking about how children learn language.

Unlike the traditional reader program, Whole Language is based on the assumption that children learn written language (reading and writing) in much the same way that they learned oral language (speaking and listening).

There are certain conditions that operate in a child's environment when he or she is learning to speak. Whole Language teachers try to duplicate those same conditions for learning to read and write.

Whole Language embraces the concept of "language across the curriculum" — meaning that no matter what content subjects are being taught (history, geography, science, health, etc.), reading and writing are incorporated into the instruction.

Materials consist of any meaningful print: library books, magazines, newspapers, textbooks, encyclopedias, dictionaries, etc.

There is no ability grouping for instruction. Children work together in large groups, small groups, pairs or individually.

There is no labeling or comparison of students. Whole Language teachers recognize that students learn at different rates and in different ways.

Teachers see themselves as facilitators whose job it is to make learning easy and interesting rather than technicians following the prescribed instructions of a basal reader program.

Reading and writing are viewed as processes to be learned rather than products to be tested.

Achievement is based on how well students can gain information from a variety of sources in a purposeful and meaningful manner and whether or not they do so.

Note: According to U. S. Department of Education statistics, the U. S. ranks 49th in world literacy. New Zealand, where 98 percent of all classrooms employ the Whole Language concept, ranks first.

Reprinted with permission from the Granite City (IL) Press Record, Feb. 8, 1990

Answers to quiz on page two:
Traditional program: 1, 4, 5, 7, 8, 10, 12, 14
Whole Language program: 2, 3, 6, 9, 11, 13

WHAT WHOLE LANGUAGE TEACHERS BELIEVE ...

- Even children appearing to know very little can learn to be good readers. If we look closely, every child has competence and knowledge that can be used effectively. Just because a child is in the lowest portion of the class does not mean he or she will have to remain there.

- Instruction in beginning reading must include massive amounts of reading and writing. Teachers must use all their ingenuity to increase reading and writing time.

- The most effective texts to support young readers do not have controlled vocabulary but present real stories with language close to the child's own. As the child increases in knowledge and understanding, texts should not only present new challenges but should always be meaningful and enjoyable.

- The most powerful teaching builds on competence instead of deficits. Programs must be designed around each child's strengths; prescriptive, inflexible programs are not adequate; skilled teaching is required.

- Instruction must be focused at the strategy level and take into account the complexities of the reading and writing processes. Children must be assisted to learn the "how to" of the reading process rather than specific, sequenced bits of information presented in isolated ways.

Pinnell, Gay, Fried, Mary and Estice, Rose. "Reading Recovery: Learning How to Make a Difference." THE READING TEACHER, Jan. 1990. Reprinted with permission.

LESSONS:
"Grabbing the teachable moment"

GRANITE CITY — The concept is simple, yet novel.

Several teachers at Parkview School are no longer breaking the school day into individual units of mathematics, science and English. Today they are teaching a series of cohesive lessons to cover each subject as part of a greater whole.

Students are being taught much the same way they learned to communicate and understand as toddlers — by taking all the parts and fitting them together as a whole.

Educators call it "grabbing the teachable moment."

The program is called Whole Language and it increasingly is being considered an innovative approach to putting American education back on track toward achievement.

Among the teachers at Parkview School in Granite City using the Whole Language approach is Phyllis Talley.

In one recent 45-minute period her third-grade class touched on geography, mathematics, history, English, research, spelling, grammar, punctuation, memory recall and, of course, reading. The lesson was about Abraham Lincoln's White House.

"Who can find Washington, D. C., on the map?" Talley asked the class.

A boy approached the map and pointed to Washington state. Another boy was called on to help. He found the right coast, but couldn't locate the city. Finally, a girl joined the search and found the capital.

"What do you know about the White House?" Talley then asked the group.

Hands shot up.

"It was once called the Presidential Palace," said one.

"The address is 1600 Pennsylvania Avenue" said another.

"It has 132 rooms and 20 bathrooms," offered another.

"It burned in … 1814," said a boy.

How many years ago was 1812?" asked Talley.

And so it went, with the lesson incorporating elements from several fields of study.

In more traditional methods of teaching, instructors would not have had the freedom to incorporate all such elements into one lesson. There was a time for math, a time for geography, a time for history, and very little overlap between subjects.

"The big plus here is that we're not tied to a rigid curriculum. We have that freedom and flexibility. It's good to feel that they (the administration) trust us as professionals," said Loretta Woolbright, a fourth-grade teacher at Parkview.

"You get to know your students better and get more involved with them," added Mary Morgan, who teaches fifth grade.

LESSONS:
"Grabbing the teachable moment"
(continued)

An integral facet of the Whole Language classroom is that students do some sort of writing exercise every day, usually tied to the rest of the day's lessons.

There is a great deal of freedom on subject matter and approach, and students are encouraged to use their imaginations. Morgan's fifth graders, for instance, wrote, scripted, designed and acted in television commercials, which were then videotaped for the class.

This circular approach, where excitement about reading leads to the desire to write, and writing leads to students sharing their works with each other, is the catalyst to keeping students — and teachers — interested in learning, say the program's proponents.

"To hear a sixth grader say, 'I love to read now, but I hated it before' — what more can you ask for?" asked sixth-grade teacher Barb Varadian.

Preliminary results gauging the success of Whole Language in the classroom seem to suggest that test scores improve. Teachers caution, however, that the impact will be more long range.

"One year of this type of learning may not make much difference, but if a student is exposed to this for two or three years or more, the concepts of researching become second nature and the habit of reading is set. As adults, they will want to continue to read," said Morgan.

"The key to this program is that it's starting from the bottom, with teachers getting excited first, and that excitement spreading upward through the administrators, rather than the administration saying to teachers, 'This is the way you will do things,' " said first-grade teacher Carole Locke.

"Kids are different these days. They know more about the world and we have to meet their needs," Varadian said.

There's a sign on Parkview Principal Nancy Marti's office wall that seems to sum up the teachers' views. It says: "If they don't learn the way you teach them, teach them the way they learn."

By Meg Tebo
Staff writer

Reprinted with permission from the Granite City (IL) Press Record, Feb. 8, 1990

CONTRASTING A WHOLE LANGUAGE PROGRAM WITH TRADITIONAL INSTRUCTION
... a writer looks back

by Meg Tebo
Staff writer Meg Tebo called upon her own experiences to compare two different types of education, basal and Whole Language.

When I was in the fifth grade, I used to sneak into the school library during my lunch hour. I'd choose a book from the shelves, settle down on the floor behind a big bookcase to avoid detection, and lose myself in another world for awhile.

Then, one day, the librarian came back early and caught me. I don't remember the specifics of the punishment, but I do remember getting kicked off of the student-librarian squad.

Even then, I knew there was something wrong with a system that would punish a kid for preferring to read a book, rather than run around outside.

There's a time and a place for everything, so they say, but instead of explaining that to me, the powers that be chose to punish me.

Later, when I was in college, I took a class that was recommended to me as both easy and interesting. We studied theories of educational policy, from Jefferson times to the present. Integral in that study was an evaluation of the "tracking" system of education.

In the tracking system, children are grouped into levels based on how quickly they learn. The inevitable result is a universal recognition of who are the "smart" kids, the "average" kids and the "dumb" or "slow" kids. The real tragedy is that these labels, once applied in about the first grade, stick with students throughout their school career.

Thus, the smart kids gain a sort of arrogance about their presumed superiority, the average kids learn not to aspire to more than average grades (or careers) and the slow kids, most tragically of all, begin to see themselves as life's losers — that they just can't cut it.

The virtual absence of that tracking system is what I find so intriguing about the Whole Language concept.

Faster students learn the topic in-depth by helping to teach it to their peers, and other students learn with less pressure from a peer than directly from a teacher. Each student is able to gain from the ideas put forth by others in a less competitive, non-threatening environment.

Teachers involved in the program say the biggest thrill for them is watching students get excited about reading; the students get excited because they have greater freedom in choosing *what* they will read.

And, the cooperative atmosphere encourages sharing that excitement by recommending favorite stories to others. That sort of excitement about reading inevitably leads to the desire to create — to write.

In the Whole Language concept, the ideas take precedence over the form. The student's imagination is allowed to create at will, and things such as grammar, spelling and punctuation are considered only after the form is on paper.

That makes sense to me. After all, you wouldn't paint the trim on your house before you paint the walls, would you?

Just as children learn to speak by listening and mimicking older human beings, so too they learn to read and to write by reading, and then by writing.

The idea becomes their own, and the final product is something of which they can be personally proud. What better motivation can there be than the satisfaction of a meaningful job well done?

Reprinted with permission from the Granite City (IL) Press Record, Feb. 8, 1990

TERMS USED IN WHOLE LANGUAGE AND LITERATURE-BASED PROGRAMS

APPROXIMATIONS

The steps learners make before achieving mastery are valued. The teacher builds on what the children know rather than concentrating on errors.

BIG BOOKS

Commercial or student-made oversized books often used in shared reading experiences where *all* children read together.

CHILD CENTERED

The learning program is determined by the needs of the child rather than by a set arbitrary curriculum which all children are expected to master at a given rate.

CHOICES

Students are encouraged to make choices of books to read, topics to explore and of other students as co-workers.

COOPERATIVE LEARNING

Extending learning and developing responsibility through work with classmates on group projects where every member of the group has specific tasks to complete. It is based on the premise that language is a social activity and facility in using language is best developed in a social setting.

DEVELOPMENTAL READINESS

Basing instruction on the demonstrated, physical, social, emotional and cognitive readiness of the learner.

EMPOWERMENT

In a whole language program teachers are considered to be professionals who make decisions for and with their students on curriculum, materials, strategies, objectives, content and evaluation.

EVALUATION

Evaluation in a whole language program is on-going and is achieved by "kidwatching". Student progress is documented through evaluation of portfolios of student work. Evaluation in a whole language program goes beyond skills acquisition to judging the learner's ability to communicate effectively.

GROUPING

The use of flexible grouping depends on need. All children have access to all materials and activities.

GUIDED READING

The teacher and students talk, think and question as they read together. The teacher acts as a facilitator, building on each child's abilities, interests and experience levels.

HOLISTIC

Providing experiences that stimulate learning in all four quadrants of the brain...content, process, feeling, creativity and appealing to all thinking and learning styles.

TERMS USED IN WHOLE LANGUAGE AND LITERATURE-BASED PROGRAMS
(continued)

IMMERSION

Providing a print-rich environment with a wide variety of ever-changing materials.

INDEPENDENT READING

Self-motivated selection and reading of books as part of every day.

INTEGRATED INSTRUCTION

The elimination of separate subjects taught in separate time slots. Instruction is built around thematic units which include all of the disciplines.

INDIVIDUALIZED READING

Each child reading a different book and working on a different task related to individual interests and abilities.

LANGUAGE EXPERIENCE

Using the child's own experiences or experiences from literature as the basis for student generated writing and reading.

LITERATURE-BASED INSTRUCTION

Using children's literature in place of the basal reader in the reading/language arts program.

MEANING-BASED READING

Reading is seen as predicting, hypothesizing and seeking meaning rather than the acquisition of isolated skills. All reading and writing activities are meaning-based.

PREDICTIVE READING

Learners are encouraged to predict action, language and structure and to make informed guesses *as* they read.

PROCESS LEARNING

An environment in which the underlying structure is the same for all students. The processes of thinking and learning are stressed.

READING ALOUD

Based on the research which shows that children who are read to show higher gains in their own reading ability. In a whole language and literature-based program students are read to many times throughout the day.

READING FOR MEANING

A reading program that stresss the meaning of any selection as contrasted with decoding of individual words.

REAL READING/WRITING

A program marked by the absence of workbooks or the teaching of isolated words or skills. Children learn to read by reading and to write by writing using real books with uncontrolled language.

TERMS USED IN WHOLE LANGUAGE AND LITERATURE-BASED PROGRAMS
(continued)

SHARED READING

The school version of the bedtime story where teacher and children read together using big books or the overhead projector, helping children enjoy books they cannot yet read fully themselves.

SKILLS

In a literature-based program skills are taught as needed and as they arise naturally from the literature.

STRATEGIES

The ways in which the learner predicts, samples, re-reads, confirms and self-corrects to gain meaning. Students in a literature-based program are helped to develop, choose and use appropriate strategies for gaining meaning.

THEMATIC UNITS

The integrated learning of reading, writing, listening, and speaking, including integration of the subject areas (math, science, art, music, social studies) in broad units of study.

WRITING PROCESS

Using the processes that real writers use...talking, writing, editing, conferencing, re-writing, revising, publishing, sharing.

Integrating the Disciplines

Steps in developing integrated thematic units (including all disciplines):

1. Select the topic or theme appropriate for the age and comprehension level of the learners.
2. Survey the school library and community for materials. Browse through materials to ascertain content and difficulty level.
3. Select activities using the materials which meet the needs of students and the demands of local or state curriculum.
4. Introduce the theme to the students. Use webbing to get student input on topics of interest to read about and investigate.
5. Provide many choices of books and activities.
6. Plan with the students for individual, small group and class projects.
7. Continual sharing, revising, adding to products. Emphasis on the processes used by students.
8. Sharing of projects. Class reviews together the learning outcomes.

Integrated Literature Studies

Topic: _____ Grade Level(s): _____

Begin with:

LITERATURE

LANGUAGE ARTS

SOCIAL STUDIES

SCIENCE

MATH

FINE ARTS

11

INTEGRATING THE DISCIPLINES

Sample Thematic Unit

BIOLOGICAL TIME
THE SECRET CLOCKS: THE
   TIME SENSES OF LIVING
   THINGS: Simon
Study tree rings, estimate the age
   of trees.
Observe animal changes, record
   observation in journals.

TIME IN NATURE

GEOLOGICAL TIM
Carbon dating
Make a map showi
   where the earth'
   oldest rocks can
   found.
Sketch soil layering
   your area.

PLACE CHANGES
THE STORY OF AN
   ENGLISH VILLAGE:
   Goodall
THE LITTLE HOUSE:
   Burton
NEW PROVIDENCE: A
   CHANGING
   CITYSCAPE: Tscharner
MISS RUMPHIUS: Cooney
Find old pictures of your
   own town.
Create a book of changes.
Adopt a place. Plan to make
   it more beautiful.

CHANGES OVER TIME

PEOPLE CHANGES
ANNIE AND THE OLD ONE: Miles
TUCK EVERLASTING: Babbit
ISLAND BOY: Cooney
SOLOMON GRUNDY: Haguet
Write epitaphs for Winnie,
   Grandmother, Solomon, Island Boy.
Draw yourself at different ages.

SEASONAL CHANGES
LEGENDS OF THE
   SUN AND THE
   MOON: Hadley
DAUGHTER OF THE
   EARTH: McDermott
Improvise scenes from
   myths, write scripts.

LONG AGO CHANGES
LIFE THROUGH THE AGES: Caselli
TIMECHANGES: Trease
THERE ONCE WAS A TIME: Ventura
"Once upon a time..."
Write a journal entry as a person living
   in another time.
Make a mural of changes over time.

PERSONAL TIME

Draw a personal timeline. Note
   important dates.
Write an autobiography.
Keep a journal.
Chart biorhythms.
MY BACKYARD HISTORY BOOK
Research family history.

TIME

TIMELY WORDS
Read poetry about time.
List idioms and other phra
   connected to TIME.
Create metaphors and sim
   to describe time.

TIME TRAVEL
TOM'S MIDNIGHT GARDEN: Pearce
FOG MAGIC: Sauer
THE CHILDREN OF GREEN KNOWE: Boston
TIME AT THE TOP: Ormondroyd
A TRAVELER IN TIME: Uttley
A STRING IN THE HARP: Bond
JEREMY VISICK: Wiseman
A GIRL CALLED BOY: Hurmence
THE ROOT CELLAR: Lunn
PLAYING BEATIE BOW: Park
Compare literary devices, settings, and
   characters.
Write sequels, different endings.
Research time periods: Are incidents in stories
   factually based?

PLAYING WITH TIME

FUTURE TIME
Z IS FOR ZACARIAH: O'Brien
A WRINKLE IN TIME: L'Engle
THE GREEN FUTURES OF TYCHO: Sleater
THE WHITE MOUNTAINS: Christopher
THIS TIME OF DARKNESS: Hoover
BREED TO COME: Norton
THE GREEN BOOK: Walsh
What is the future of our planet?
Study issues relating to animal extinction,
   environment, nuclear war.
What inventions are likely to change the
   future?
Write your own science fiction story.

Sample unit from: AN INTEGRATED LANGUAGE PERSPECTIVE IN THE ELEMENTARY SCHOOL by Christine
Pappas, Barbara Z. Kiefer and Linda S. Levstik. Longman, 1990. Included with permission

TIME PASSING

FROM DAY TO DAY

WHAT MAKES DAY AND NIGHT: Branley
Compare and contrast the use of time in these
    books.
Make a cartoon or film strip to show the passage of
    time.
THE HOUSE FROM MORNING TO NIGHT: Bour
MORNING, NOON AND NIGHTTIME,
    TOO:Hopkins
DAWN: Shulevitz
FOG DRIFT MORNING: Ray
DUSK TO DAWN: Hill
NIGHT IN THE COUNTRY: Rylant
Sketch or paint your favorite time of day. Choose
    music to capture your mood.

THE WAY TO START A DAY: Baylor
WHEN THE SKY WAS LIKE LACE: Horwitz
Write rules for your favorite time of day.
PORCUPINE STEW: Major
HILDILID'S NIGHT: Ryan
GRANDFATHER TWILIGHT: Berger
Write about a magical event.

OPENING NIGHT: Isadora
NIGHT GHOSTS AND HERMITS: Stolz
NIGHT MARKETS: Horwitz
Interview someone who works at night.
View night creatures at the zoo.

FROM SEASON TO SEASON

MY FAVORITE TIME OF
    YEAR: Pearson
SUGARING TIME: Laskey
TIME OF WONDER: McCloskey
OX-CART MAN: Cooney
Survey people's favorite times of
    year.
Compare hours of daylight and
    dark at different times of year.

TIME IN MUSIC

Grofé, "Sunset" and "Sunrise"
    from Grand Canyon Suite
Ravel, "Day Break" from Daphnis
    et Chloe
Prokofiev, "Midnight Waltz" from
    Cinderella
Vivaldi, The Four Seasons

TIME IN ART

French Impressionists Monet
Sunset Impressions, Haystacks
Sisley, June Morning
American Luminists — Heade,
    Twilight, Sprouting Rock
    Beach
Church, Morning in the Tropics

Other Artists —
Van Gogh, Starry Night
Turner, Norham Castle, Sunset
Constable, Clouds
Hopper, Night Hawks, Night
Shadows

MEASURING TIME

MUSICAL CLOCKS
metronomes
notation system

SIMPLE CLOCKS
Make sundials,
sand clocks,
water clocks,
13 CLOCKS: Thurber
MS. GLEE WAS WAITING: Hill
CLOCKS AND MORE
    CLOCKS:Hutchins
CLOCKS AND HOW THEY GO:Gibbons

Make a graffiti wall of time words.
Compose accompaniment for TIME
    poems.

THE IDEAS OF EINSTEIN: Fisher
IT'S ALL RELATIVE: Apfel
Study the theory of relativity.

MECHANICAL CLOCKS
Bring time pieces from
    home, sketch and
    describe them.

INTEGRATING THE DISCIPLINES
Sample Thematic Unit

BIOLOGICAL TIME
THE SECRET CLOCKS: THE
   TIME SENSES OF LIVING
   THINGS: Simon
Study tree rings, estimate the age
   of trees.
Observe animal changes, record
   observation in journals.

TIME IN NATURE

SCIENCE

GEOLOGICAL TIM
Carbon dating
Make a map showin
   where the earth's
   oldest rocks can b
   found.
Sketch soil layering
   your area.

PLACE CHANGES
THE STORY OF AN
   ENGLISH VILLAGE:
   Goodall
THE LITTLE HOUSE:
   Burt

SOCIAL
STUDIES

NEW P
CHA
   CITYSCAPE: Tscharner
MISS RUMPHIUS: Cooney
Find old pictures of your
   own town.
Create a book of changes.
Adopt a place. Plan to make
   it more beautiful.

CHANGES OVER TIME

PEOPLE CHANGES
ANNIE AND THE OLD ONE: Miles
TUCK EVERLASTING: Babbit
ISLAND BOY: Cooney
SOLOMON GRUNDY: Haguet
Write epitaphs for Winnie,
   Grandmother, Solomon, Island Boy.
Draw yourself at different ages.

SEASONAL CHANGES
LEGENDS OF THE
   SUN AND THE
   MOON: Hadley
DAUGHTER OF THE
   EARTH: McDermott
Improvise scenes from
   myths, write scripts.

LONG AGO CHANGES
LIFE THROUGH THE AGES: Caselli
TIMECHANGES: Trease
THERE ONCE WAS A TIME: Ventura
"Once upon a time…"
Write a journal entry as a person living
   in anothe
Make a mural of changes over time.

MATH

TIME

PERSONAL TIME

Draw a personal timeline. Note
   import
Write an autobiography.
Keep a journal.
Chart biorhythms.
MY BACKYARD HISTORY BOOK
Research family history.

SCIENCE

TIME TRAVEL
TOM'S MIDNIGHT GARDEN: Pearce
FOG MAGIC: Sauer
THE CHILDREN OF GREEN KNOWE: Boston
TIME AT THE TOP: Ormondroyd
A TRAVELER IN TIME: Uttley
A STRING IN THE HARP: Bond
JEREMY VISICK: Wiseman
A GIRL CALLED BOY: Hurmence
THE ROOT CELLAR: Lunn
PLAYING BEATIE BOW: Park
Compare literary devices, settings, and
   characters.
Write sequels, different endings.
Research time periods: Are incidents in stories
   factually based?

SOCIAL
STUDIES

TIMELY WORDS
Read poetry about time.
List idioms and other phras
   connected to TIME.
Create metaphors and simi
   to describe time.

PLAYING WITH TIME

SCIENCE

FUTURE TIME
Z IS FOR ZACARIAH: O'Brien
A WRINKLE IN TIME: L'Engle
THE GREEN FUTURES OF TYCHO: Sleater
THE WHITE MOUNTAINS: Christopher
THIS TIME OF DARKNESS: Hoover
BREED TO COME: Norton
THE GREEN BOOK: Walsh
What is the future of our planet?
Study issues relating to animal extinction,
   environment, nuclear war.
What inventions are likely to change the
   future?
Write your own science fiction story.

TIME PASSING

FROM DAY TO DAY
WHAT MAKES DAY AND NIGHT: Branley
Compare and contrast the use of time in these
    books.
Make a cartoon or film strip to show the passage of
    time.

[SCIENCE]

THE HOUSE FROM MORNING TO NIGHT: Bour
MORNING, NOON AND NIGHTTIME,
    TOO: Hopkins

DAW[ART]
FOG DRIFT MORNING: Ray
DUSK TO DAWN: Hill
NIGHT IN THE COUNTRY: Rylant
Sketch or paint your favorite time of day. Choose
    music to capture your mood.

THE WAY TO START A DAY: Baylor
WHEN THE SKY WAS LIKE LACE: Horwitz
Write rules for your favorite time of day.
PORCU[SOCIAL STUDIES]
HILDIL
GRAND   HT: Berger
Write about a magical event.

OPENING NIGHT: Isadora
NIGHT GHOSTS AND HERMITS: Stolz
NIGHT MARKETS: Horwitz
Interview someone who works at night.
View night creatures at the zoo.

FROM SEASON TO SEASON
MY FAVORITE TIME OF
    YEAR: Pearson
SUGARING TIME: Laskey
TIME OF WONDER: McCloskey
OX-CART MAN: Cooney
Survey people's favorite times of
    year.
Compare hours of daylight and
    dark at different times of year.

TIME IN MUSIC
Grofé, "Sunset" and "Sunrise"
    from Grand Canyon Suite
Ravel,   [MUSIC]   Daphnis
    et C
Prokofiev, "Midnight Waltz" from
    Cinderella
Vivaldi, The Four Seasons

TIME IN ART
French Impressionists Monet
Sunset Impressions, Haystacks
Sisley, June Morning
Amer[ART]Heade,
    Tw   ck
    Beach
Church, Morning in the Tropics

Other Artists —
Van Gogh, Starry Night
Turner, Norham Castle, Sunset
Constable, Clouds
Hopper, Night Hawks, Night
Shadows

MEASURING TIME

MUSICAL CLOCKS
metronomes
notat[MUSIC]

SIMPLE CLOCKS
Make sundials,
sand clocks,
water clocks,
13 CLOCKS: Thurber
MS. GLEE WAS WAITING: Hill
CLOCKS AND MORE
    CLOCKS: Hutchins
CLOCKS AND HOW THEY GO: Gibbons

[MATH]

Make a graffit   s.
Compose accompaniment for TIME
    poems.

THE IDEAS OF EINSTEIN: Fisher
IT'S ALL RELATIVE: Apfel
Study the theory of relativity.

MECHANICAL CLOCKS
Bring time pieces from
home, sketch and
describe them.

[SCIENCE]

LITERATURE-BASED READING INSTRUCTION

What research says:

> *Children enrolled in a reading/literature program using trade books without fixed vocabulary or sentence length...followed by meaning-related activities, showed significant increases over a group using only the basal program in word knowledge, reading comprehension and quality of vocabulary.*
> Cohen, Dorothy. "The Effect of Literature on Vocabulary and Reading Achievement". ELEMENTARY ENGLISH (Feb. 1968)
>
> *This carefully developed experimental study showed that "the use of children's literature to teach children to read had a positive effect on students' achievement and attitudes toward reading...much greater than children taught in a traditional program".*
> Eldredge, J. Lloyd. "Alternatives to Traditional Reading Instruction". THE READING TEACHER (Oct. 1986)

READING IS A LIFESTYLE NOT A SKILL

OBJECTIVE: To explore and/or reaffirm the concept of reading as a dynamic, interactive process of constructing meaning; of changing the way we ask questions; of recognizing the importance of visualization in the reading process; and to examine alternate methods of reading instruction including whole class instruction and partnership reading.

A WHOLE LANGUAGE APPROACH:

- Begins with the sharing of a whole story, poem or song.
- Redefines reading as predicting, questioning and seeking meaning rather than word recognition.
- Surrounds children with print.
- Uses all forms of communication: reading, writing, speaking, art, music, drama.
- Encourages understanding of ideas and patterns.
- Develops skills naturally from text as needed.
- Allows time for individualized reading.
- Offers flexible grouping...uses cooperative and/or partnership reading.

Traditional instruction begins with **letters** and finally moves to story.

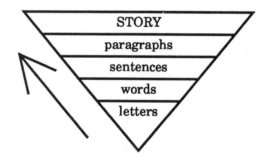

A LITERATURE BASED READING PROGRAM:

- Suggests that children acquire abilities through experiences with whole text! Books are used with natural, uncontrolled language.
- Uses the neurological impress method..reading aloud or with music in unison..pointing to words and repeating them as they are read.
- Builds in time for reading aloud to students.
- Permits time for silent sustained reading.
- Is affective....emphasizes changing attitudes toward reading.
- Allows for self selection of reading materials.
- Teaches skills always in meaningful context.
- Stresses process writing and other output activities.

Whole-language instruction begins with **story** and finally moves to letters.

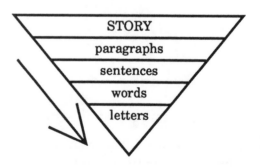

NANCY POLETTE'S LITERATURE-BASED
READING GUIDE Copyright © 1991

Pre-Reading Strategies:

1 **Categorizing New Vocabulary:** Presenting a list of new words in the story. Students work together to group the words in whatever categories they choose. Grouping defines!

2 **Creative Thinking:** Brainstorming possible characters, actions, and problems that may arise in a story (fluency), unique solutions to problems (flexibility/originality) and elaborating on settings and character descriptions. Students use decision grids in creative problem-solving.

3 **Paragraph Construction:** Showing one illustration from the story. On separate slips of paper, groups of students write words related to the illustration. Words are then arranged in a topic sentence. More words are arranged to make sentences giving details to create a paragraph.

4 **Pre-Reading Journal:** Writing in individual journals for five to seven minutes on topics or sentence starters related to the story. These are shared orally. The writing is done *before* reading the story.

5 **Predicting Vocabulary in the Story:** Presenting the story title and a list of words that might be in the story. Children predict which words will be in the story and listen carefully to see if they were right.

6 **Topic Talking:** Assigning partners. The teacher states a topic. Partner A talks to Partner B on the topic until the teacher says "switch". Partner B talks until the teacher says "stop". Introduce another topic. Gradually increase the time children talk and the size of the group. Variation: Let B tell A what A said.

7 **Topic Focusing:** Listing what is known and what we think we know but aren't sure about, comparing lists and then reading about the topic to support or deny guesses.

During Reading:

8 **Concert Reading:** In the primary grades this means reading aloud poetry to the rhythm of music (impressing language patterns on the brain). Upper grade students select music that fits the mood of the literature and read aloud short selections.

9 **Shared Reading:** Teacher and students reading aloud together both prose and poetry. Choose books or poems with repeating patterns so that the reading disabled can join in.

10 **Predictive Reading:** Asking questions as reading progresses and predicting both action and outcomes.

11 **Partnership Reading:** Each student is reading a different book (independent reading) and has a reading partner. The teacher calls "stop" after several pages are read silently. Partners summarize story action to this point for each other and predict what will happen next. Reading continues until finished. Partners summarize again.

12 **Readers Theatre:** Reading a story as a play and interpreting action and feeling with the voice.

13 **Attentive and Critical Listening:** Giving specific words, topics or situations to listen for as the story is read orally (attentive listening), often students are asked to make a decision or judgement based on what they have heard (critical listening).

14 **Critical Reading:** Reading for data which supports a writer's premise or reading "between the lines" to determine whether missing information is essential to making a judgement or decision. Requires a high level of analysis of data.

After Reading:

15 Sequencing: Using story strips, students work together to put them in order. Variation: Strips can need capitalization and punctuation which students add.

16 Comprehension Games: Using the "I Have, Who Has" game in which each student has an "I Have", "Who Has" card with information from the story. Promotes careful listening.

17 Questions to Ask After Reading: Asking divergent questions that get somewhere. How many ways? What if? If you were? Suppose that? How is _____ like _____ ? Training older students to follow the reflective questioning model using objective, reflective, interpretative and decisional types of questions.

18 Comparing Tales: There are no two stories that can't be compared! Ask: How is the story we have just read like (mention any other tale the students might know). Think of at least twenty likenesses.

19 Word Banks: Compiling lists of words within similar categories and related to the selection which students keep in their notebooks to use for their own writing.

20 Summarizing in Poetry and Song: Writing or completing a partially written story or song about the reading selection which is then performed by the group.

21 Vocabulary Games: Friendly contests where teams respond to illustrations from a story by listing all of a particular kind of word or words within a given time limit.

22 Skills from the Text: Introducing any skill (Example: words with prefixes) by challenging students to find and read aloud a sentence from the story which contains the skill.

23 Skills from Story Illustrations: Testing the students' knowledge or ability to apply a particular skill. Asking students to write sentences based on an illustration from the story which contain specific items (Example: homonym, adverbs that tell how, a direct object, etc.).

24 Storyboards: Reconstructing a story or writing a sequel by moving incident cards on a ten space story board until all story elements work together. An excellent vehicle for rehearsing and discussing before writing.

25 Analyzing Literary Style: Re-reading sections of a story to find elements of style. (Example: simile, alliteration, hyperbole, allusion, metaphor, repetition etc.).

26 Writing Patterns/Book Reports: Using patterns from literature as models for students' own creative writing. Using poetry patterns for reporting on books read.

27 Research Models: Reporting on non-fiction topics that arise from a story by using models that discourage copying … the True/False Book, the Bio-Poem, etc.

28 Research Organizer: Selecting a topic, a thinking skill to use in dealing with the topic and a product which will result from the research.

READING STRATEGIES
What to do when it doesn't make sense!

Read it again!

Sometimes reading a sentence a second time will help to clarify the meaning.

Go on Reading

The sentences which follow sometimes explain a puzzling word or phrase.

Use Picture Clues

If the reading selection has illustrations, look carefully at the pictures to see if you can make sense out of the text.

Substitute a Word

Put another word *that makes sense* in place of the strange word.

Skip the Word or Phrase

If you have the general meaning of the reading selection and understand the sentences or paragraphs which follow then skip the puzzling word.

Look it up

If you go on reading *but* the sentence or paragraphs that follow don't make sense, then it is time to look up the word in the dictionary.

CATEGORIZING VOCABULARY ▣

Grades 1-3

Giving students a purpose and focus for reading

The Seven Chinese Brothers
by Margaret Mahy

Introduce the vocabulary for the literature selection

Here are words we will meet in the story. Put a 1 in front of each word that is a *person*. Put a 2 in front of each word that is a *place*. Put a 3 in front of each word that is a *thing*. Guess if you do not know!

___	Ch'in Shih Huang	___	wall
___	emperor	___	mountains
___	China	___	bones
___	Brother	___	iron
___	fly	___	legs
___	miles	___	fires
___	teardrop	___	village

Introduce the literature

The Seven Chinese Brothers
by Margaret Mahy
Illus. by Jean and Mou-sien Tseng
Scholastic, 1990

Once upon a time when Ch'in Shih Huang was emperor of all China, there lived seven brothers, each with an amazing power all his own. First Brother could hear a fly sneeze from a hundred miles away. Second Brother could spot that very fly sneezing away on the Great Wall of China. Third Brother lifted mountains that got in his way. Fourth Brother had bones of iron and Fifth Brother, legs that grew. Sixth Brother kept warm by sitting in fires, and Seventh Brother always tried to stay cheerful — because when he was unhappy, it took him only a single teardrop to drown an entire village!

Students read to support or deny guesses

CATEGORIZING VOCABULARY ▣
Grades 4-8
Giving students a purpose and focus for reading

Here are some numbered categories:
1. people   2. places   3. equipment   4. aircraft
5. groups   6. defense strategies   7. offense strategies

Introduce the vocabulary for the literature selection

After each word below, write the number of the heading under which it should belong. Then read about the Battle of Britain to confirm or deny choices.

__ Air raid shelter   __ Axis   __ Allies
__ Blenheims   __ Convoy   __ Dorniers
__ Incendiaries   __ London   __ Luftwaffe
__ Spitfires   __ Wardens   __ Britain
__ Invasion   __ Goering   __ Blackout
__ Coventry   __ Blitzkrieg   __ Home guard
__ Jerry   __ Lorries   __ RAF
__ Stukas   __ Hitler   __ High command
__ Raids   __ Radar

Introduce the literature

The Ghosts of War by Daniel Cohen, Putnam, 1990
The settings of these spine-chilling stories include ancient Greece, medieval Japan, 17th-century England, and New York City during the Second World War. There are haunted battlefields, soldiers' premonitions of death, strange encounters with ghostly pilots, and a haunted prisoner of war camp where unexplained sounds were picked up by a tape recorder. Tales feature the troubled spirit of a Polish mercenary, the headless Lady of Recruit House, and the "cursed car" that brought disaster to all its owners.

Students read to support or deny guesses

An introduction to one of the stories in: *The Ghosts of War* by Daniel Cohen

The Blitzkrieg had ended. The wheels of lorries carrying the injured no longer turned in the streets of London or Coventry. The home guard welcomed the respite from seeking injured buried under buildings hit with incendiaries from the Stuka Bombers of Hitler's Luftwaffe. But the German Dorniers and Stukas were still in the air! Captain Brick Barton knew them well after more than three years as an RAF pilot flying anything that would fly...Blenheims, Spitfires and B24s. But by 1943, things had changed. It was England's turn to bomb Germany.

Brick Barton was one of the B24 pilots suiting up on this night for one of the dangerous bombing runs. His co-pilot was a young Lieutenant on his first combat mission. The night was to end like no other ... the RAF crews still whisper about it.

CREATIVE THINKING: INTRODUCING A PICTURE BOOK 🔲

The Seven Chinese Brothers by Margaret Mahy Scholastic, 1990

Fluency: The ability to make many responses.
   Name all the words you can think of that have anything to do with China.

Flexibility: Finding new categories. Stretching the mind beyond the expected response.
   How can you group the items you named under fluency?

Originality: Responding in new or original ways.
   What group and/or items did you name that no one else named?

Elaboration: Adding details to make a product more complete.
   In this story the Emperor wants to build a very long, high wall to protect th[e] people from invaders. What could you add to the wall to make it more usefu[l] or attractive?

Planning: Determining a task to be done, the steps to take, materials needed and possible problems.
   In the story of *The Seven Chinese Brothers*, Seventh Brother always tried t[o] stay cheerful, because when he was unhappy, it took him only a single teardrop to drown an entire village. Pretend you are one of the Brothers. Make a plan to keep Seventh Brother happy.

Forecasting: Determining cause and effect.
   What would cause an Emperor to build a very long wall between his countr[y] and another country? What effect will this wall have on the people of both countries?

Decision Making and Problem Solving
   A. Examine the facts
   C. List alternatives
   E. Score alternatives on a decision grid

   B. State the problem
   D. List criteria for judging alternatives
   F. State solution

In this story the Emperor becomes so angry that he orders that one of the brothers will be shot full of arrows on the next morning. He is put in prison and well guarded. His other brothers want to save him. What can they do?

	Criteria				Total
Score: 1 = no 2 = maybe 3 = yes **Alternatives**	*Needs to be fast.*				
Ask Emperor to release him.					

Evaluation: Judging the pros and cons of an item or situation.

CREATIVE THINKING: INTRODUCING NOVELS

T. J. and the Pirate Who Wouldn't Go Home by Carol Gorman
Scholastic, 1990

Fluency: The ability to make many responses.
> Uncle Ainsley is always inventing things. Many of his inventions get him into trouble. Name all the real inventors you can.

Flexibility: Finding new categories. Stretching the mind beyond the expected response.
> How can you group the items you named under fluency?

Originality: Responding in new or original ways.
> What group and/or items did you name that no one else named?

Elaboration: Adding details to make a product more complete.
> Select one everyday item (comb, toothbrush, pencil, etc.) What could you add to the item to make it more interesting or useful?

Planning: Determining a task to be done, the steps to take, materials needed and possible problems.
> Instead of sending himself into the past with his new time machine, Uncle Ainsley has accidentally brought a pirate to the present. The pirate likes to steal from stores and pick people's pockets. Plan a way for Uncle Ainsley to keep the pirate busy at home while he fixes the time machine.

Forecasting: Determining cause and effect.
> What might be the causes of seeing a pirate walk down the street in your city/town? What would be the effects of having a pickpocket/burglarizing pirate loose in your city or town?

Decision Making and Problem Solving
> A. Examine the facts
> B. State the problem
> C. List alternatives
> D. List criteria for judging alternatives
> E. Score alternatives on a decision grid
> F. State solution

Uncle Ainsley fixes the time machine and is ready to send the pirate, Captain Billy, back to the 17th century. But, Captain Billy likes game shows, TV and Big Macs. He doesn't want to go back. What will T. J. and his uncle do?

		— Criteria —				Total
Score: 1 = no 2 = maybe 3 = yes **Alternatives**	*Needs to be fast.*					
Call the police.						

Evaluation: Judging the pros and cons of an item or situation.

CREATIVE THINKING ▣

Fluency: The ability to make many responses.

Flexibility: Finding new categories. Stretching the mind beyond the expected response.
How can you group the items you named under fluency?

Originality: Responding in new or original ways.
What group and/or items did you name that no one else named?

Elaboration: Adding details to make a product more complete.

Planning: Determining a task to be done, the steps to take, materials needed and possible problems.

Forecasting: Determining cause and effect.

Decision Making and Problem Solving
A. Examine the facts
B. State the problem
C. List alternatives
D. List criteria for judging alternatives
E. Score alternatives on a decision grid
F. State solution

	——— Criteria ———					Total
Score: 1 = no 2 = maybe 3 = yes **Alternatives**						

Evaluation: Judging the pros and cons of an item or situation.

A PROBLEM SOLVING MODEL

Every story has a problem that must be solved. Read a story to the point where the problem arises. *Before* finishing the story to see how the author solves the problem, try solving the problem yourself by using the steps listed below. Then finish the story. Did you like your solution better? The author's? Were they the same?

1. What important facts can you state about the situation?

_____

_____

_____

2. State the major problem.

_____

_____

3. List as many ways as you can to deal with the problem. These are your alternatives.

_____

_____

_____

_____

_____

4. Select the four best ideas and enter them on the decision grid below.

5. Two criteria for judging ideas are provided in the grid. Add a third of your own.

6. Evaluate each idea on a scale of one to five. A poor rating is one; a high rating is five.

Title _____

Author _____

Story Problem: _____

_____

_____

_____

Scale 1-5 Best Ideas	Is It Fast?	Is It Low Cost?	Yours

PARAGRAPH CONSTRUCTION ▨

Responding to a visual

PROCEDURE:

1. Make an overhead transparency of the visual.

2. Display the visual and ask students to list name words, describing words and action words related to the visual. Provide students with small 'postits' or slips of paper so that each word can be written on a separate piece of paper. Students can work alone or in small groups with each member of the group contributing a word in turn.

3. When students have large banks of words, ask them to select from their word banks those words which will make a sentence describing the picture. Explain that this is a topic sentence.

4. Encourage students to share their completed sentences orally.

5. Challenge students to use other words in their word banks to add one or more details about the picture in sentence form. Explain that a paragraph contains a topic sentence and other sentences that add details about the topic. Allow sufficient time for students to develop their sentences.

6. Share the story from which the visual is taken.

PRE-READING JOURNALS
Grades 4-8

One method which has proven effective in giving students a purpose and focus for reading is the pre-reading journal. Using this method, students respond to provocative questions dealing with plot or theme of a particular story, chapter or novel before reading the selection. After writing for about five minutes, students are encouraged to share what they have written orally. This is an ideal way to pull from the experiences of older students in preparing to read.

Advantages of pre-reading journals

Since journals are not graded for spelling, punctuation, etc., students can write freely about topics, discovering what they think or how they feel about the topic.

The lively discussion which follows is fueled by the free-writing experiences and prepares students for the selection to be read.

The daily writing activity and subsequent discussion helps students to become better readers as student interest in a topic is generated and students focus on concepts and ideas which will be presented in the reading.

For reluctant readers, the free writing time is a non-threatening way to prepare students for what they will be reading.

When students are allowed to concentrate on what to write rather than how to write it, higher quality responses often occur, reading becomes more relevant and students become better readers.

Sample open ended sentence starters for the pre-reading journal experience:

T. J. and the Pirate Who Wouldn't Go Home
by Carol Gorman, Scholastic, 1990

Chapter One:
1. Falling asleep in class can be...
2. When the teacher has a black belt in karate ...
3. Hearing the sound of splintering glass at night ...
4. Meeting a real pirate could be ...

Chapter Two:
1. Trying to explain seeing a pirate burglarize a TV store ...
2. Eccentric means ...
3. Trying out a time machine could be ...

Sharing responses

Volunteers can share responses or students can be placed in small groups where every student shares his/her response with the group.

Adapted from: Pre-reading Journal article by Patricia F. Hunter appearing in the WRITING TEACHER Aug/ Sep 88. Included with permission of the WRITING TEACHER.

PREDICTING VOCABULARY

Grades 1-3

The story of *The Seven Chinese Brothers* takes place in China. Here are words we might *expect* to find in the story. *Predict* which words will be in the story by writing after each word **Y** for Yes, **N** for No and **M** for Maybe.

1. Emperor ____
2. teacup ____
3. mountain ____
4. village ____
5. stones ____
6. General ____
7. sword ____
8. archers ____
9. river ____
10. earthquake ____
11. fishes ____

Answer: All of the words appear in the story except for #2. (This activity promotes attentive listening).

TOPIC TALKING
Primary and Upper Grades

1. Assign partners
2. State a topic.
3. Partner A talks on the topic to B until you say "Switch" (after 10 seconds)
4. Partner B talks on the same topic until you say "Stop". (10 seconds)
5. Follow the procedure with a second topic (30 seconds) and a third topic (one minute).
6. Over a period of time slowly increase the amount of time *and* the size of the group.

Teacher Guidelines for Topic Talking:

1. Topics should be those that students know something about.
2. Topics can be assigned and time allowed for preparation.
3. As students become comfortable with Topic Talking, increase the group size to three, then four, etc. As groups increase in size only one or two students will do topic talking for that class period.
4. As a variation of the procedure above, try this: Student A speaks to Student B on a topic for the allotted time. When you say "Switch", Student B tells Student A what he or she said until you say "Stop".
5. This activity can be used at any grade level. Topics for elementary grades should always be concrete in nature. Topics for middle school/ junior high students can be abstract (Example: time, beauty, etc.)

TOPIC TALKING: A Variation
Appropriate for all grade levels
(The illustration used will vary depending on the interests and maturity level of the students.)

Oral Descriptions:
A Pre-Reading Activity for Picture Books

1. Assign partners.

2. Using a big book or large illustration from the picture book ask Partner A to describe for Partner B what he/she is seeing.
   Tell:
   > Who is in the picture?
   > What is the setting?
   > What is the mood of the picture?
   > What is happening?
   > What do you think might happen next?

   Only Partner A is looking at the picture. Partner B has eyes closed.

3. Show another illustration from the story. This time Partner B tells what he/she sees using the guidelines above but in addition tells whether he/she believes this illustration comes before or after the illustration described by Partner A and why.

4. Following the oral descriptions both pictures can be viewed and discussed. Points in discussion might include the illustrator's use of:
   > Line
   > Shapes
   > Framing devices
   > Perspective

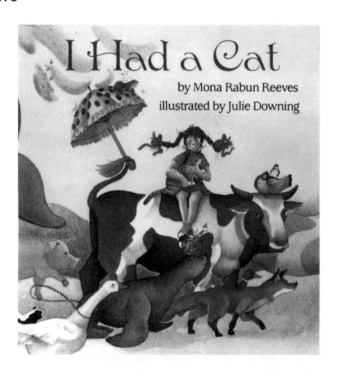

Illustration from *I Had a Cat* by Mona Rabun Reeves. Illus. by Julie Downing, MacMillan, 1989. Included with permission.

TOPIC FOCUSING

Grades 4-8

Reading Non-Fiction With Purpose and Focus

Topic: The Statue of Liberty

1. List what you know about the topic.

Location: _____
Gift from : _____
Cost: _____
Made of : _____
Height: _____
Weight: _____
Designed by: _____
Purpose: _____

2. List what you think you know but aren't sure.

Location: _____
Gift from : _____
Cost: _____
Made of : _____
Height: _____
Weight: _____
Designed by: _____
Purpose: _____

3. Share lists. Do they agree? Disagree?

_____
_____
_____

4. Read!

After Reading:

1. Examine the information previously listed.
2. Star correct responses.
3. Check incorrect responses.
4. Place a question mark by responses that were neither confirmed nor denied in the article (These may be possible research items.)
5. What new questions arise as a result of reading?
6. Where can you find the answers?

TOPIC FOCUSING

Reading Non-Fiction With Purpose and Focus

Topic: _____

1. List what you
   know about the
   topic.
   _____
   _____
   _____
   _____
   _____
   _____
   _____
   _____

2. List what you
   think you know
   but aren't sure.
   _____
   _____
   _____
   _____
   _____
   _____
   _____

3. Share lists.
   Do they agree?
   Disagree?
   _____
   _____
   _____

4. Read!

After Reading:
1. Examine the information previously listed.
2. Star correct responses.
3. Check incorrect responses.
4. Place a question mark by responses that were neither
   confirmed nor denied in the article (These may be
   possible research items.)
5. What new questions arise as a result of reading?
6. Where can you find the answers?

INTRODUCTION: 🔳
About Concert Reading (Reading With Music)
by Nancy Polette
Grades 1-3 Rhythm Reading / Grades 4-8 Mood Reading

What is concert reading?

Concert Reading is reading aloud to the rhythm or mood of music.

Why do concert reading?

When the reader uses music as a background for oral reading the words flow from the page with expression and feeling. It is a way to get beyond the mere words of a passage to the images and emotions that underlie the selection. Concert reading well done is, as its name implies, a performance. It becomes an enjoyable experience when the reader blends his or her voice with the author's words and the music. The entire literary experience is enhanced for both the reader and the listener.

What is rhythm reading?

Begin with primary children in doing nursery rhymes to march tunes or rhythm pieces. This is one method of neurological impressioning, a method of teaching reading which is highly recommended. In impressing the language on the brain with rhythm and music, it is often surprising how well young children can read a selection when the music is taken away. Begin with familiar rhymes and have the words on an overhead transparency or on the story chart. Even though the children may know the verse it is important that they see the words as they say them. Those children who may have difficulty at first will soon chime in.

How do I select music to read to?

There are only four basic moods of music: happy, sad, scary and peaceful. The fast or slow pace of the music determines the degree of the mood, that is, a piece can be a little scary (slower pace) or extremely scary (louder, faster pace). As one becomes familiar with the works of a variety of composers an association can often be made between a particular composer and his music. Beethoven, for example, often presents a somber, serious mood in his music. Schumann's music is frequently lighter or more reflective.

When you have determined the mood of the literary selection then listen to several music selections. Intuitively you will *feel* which selection is right for the piece. Students in grades four through high school are usually very good at matching music to the mood of a reading, perhaps because of the extensive television mood music they hear.

Rhythm Reading Steps

1. Read the poem aloud without music.

2. Tap your fingers (or your toes) to feel the "beat" or rhythm of the poem.

3. Listen to the march music on your tape or record player. Does it have the same rhythm?

4. Read the poem to the rhythm of the music.
   (Use a big voice!)
   (Read with feeling!)

A Snake in the Schoolroom
by Nancy Polette

A snake in the schoolroom?
Oh, climb on your chairs!
The teacher is tending
To outside affairs.
The children are screaming
And making a din
And chasing the snake,
When guess who walks in?
The principal's angry,
He frowns and he scowls.
"Where is your teacher?"
The principal howls.
"Let us have order,
Get back in your seats!
You will not get recess
Nor after-lunch treats."
Then the principal started
To do a strange dance.
(And we all knew why.)
There's a snake
In his pants!

Henry and the Bear
by Nancy Polette

Henry J. O'Higgins
   Had a bear in his chair,
And he called
   The local conservation man. (Oh, yes!)

"Get that growling bear outside!"
   Henry J. O'Higgins cried,
"Get it out of here
   As fast, as fast as you can!" (I guess!)

The man looked at the beast
   Ready for a human feast,
And he took off
   Like a rocket in the night.
      (What a mess!)
So...Henry J. O'Higgins
   Has a bear in his chair,
And Henry, not the bear
   Has taken flight! (one less!)

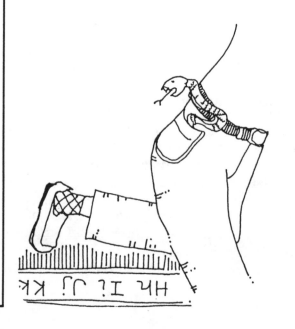

CONCERT READING: Grades 4-8
Mood Reading

Mood Reading Steps

1. Decide on the mood of a story or poem. (Happy, sad, peaceful, scary)

2. Choose music that has the same mood.

3. Read aloud with the music playing softly in the background.

TOMORROW - (A Fable)

In the Land of the Great Beyond, beside the golden gates, two women met. One was a strong and beautiful spirit with shining garments and a face full of clear light. But the other was little, and pinched and gray and she trembled with fright.

"Why do you tremble?" asked the first woman. "I am afraid," said the second. "It is all so strange here. I have no home, no friends and I am alone and frightened."

"That is strange," said the strong spirit. "I never felt so at home before. Everything is friendly to my eyes. The very trees are as if I had known them always."

"Let me hold your hand," begged the frightened one. "I shall perhaps not be so afraid if I am with you. I was a great lady on earth. I lived in a fine house with riches and jewels and servants to care for me. Yet, I had to leave them all in haste and come to this strange place. It was terrible! Was it the same with you?"

"No," said the other, "I came willingly."

The frightened woman clung to the other and peered in her face. "Tell me," she cried, "did we ever meet on Earth? Your face is not only friendly, it is familiar. It is as if I had seen you often, yet none of the noble ladies I knew had such grace and strength. Who were you, kind spirit?"

"I was your washerwoman," said the other.

ATTENTIVE LISTENING 13
Comprehension Game 16

An "I Have, Who Has?" game can be constructed for any story. The example given here is for the story, "Tomorrow" found on the previous page. Cut apart the boxes and distribute randomly about the class. The student with the starred card reads the WHO HAS portion of the card. By listening carefully, students should be able to respond correctly even if they have not read the story.

I HAVE: "I was your washerwoman". WHO HAS: Where does the story "Tomorrow" take place? *	I HAVE: The strong woman felt at home where everything was friendly. WHO HAS: What did the frightened woman ask of the strong woman?
I HAVE: "Tomorrow" takes place in the Land of the Great Beyond. WHO HAS: Where did the two women meet?	I HAVE: The frightened woman asked to hold the strong woman's hand. WHO HAS: What was the frightened woman's life like on earth?
I HAVE: The two women met by the golden gates. WHO HAS: What did the two women look like?	I HAVE: On earth the frightened woman was a rich lady with jewels and servants. WHO HAS: How did the frightened woman feel about coming to this new place?
I HAVE: One woman was strong and beautiful and the other was pinched and gray. WHO HAS: How did the pinched and gray woman feel?	I HAVE: The frightened woman did not want to come. She felt terrible. WHO HAS: How did the strong woman feel about coming to this strange new place?
I HAVE: The pinched and gray woman trembled with fright. WHO HAS: Why was the gray woman afraid?	I HAVE: The strong woman came willingly. WHO HAS: What did the frightened woman notice about the strong woman?
I HAVE: The gray woman was afraid of being alone in a strange place. WHO HAS: How did the strong woman feel?	I HAVE: The frightened woman thought she had met the strong woman before. WHO HAS: How did the strong woman identify herself?

FORM FOR THE "I Have, Who Has?" MODEL

I HAVE: ** Start here: WHO HAS:	I HAVE: WHO HAS:
I HAVE: WHO HAS:	I HAVE: WHO HAS:
I HAVE: WHO HAS:	I HAVE: WHO HAS:
I HAVE: WHO HAS:	I HAVE: WHO HAS:
I HAVE: WHO HAS:	I HAVE: WHO HAS:
I HAVE: WHO HAS:	I HAVE: WHO HAS:
I HAVE: WHO HAS:	I HAVE: WHO HAS:

SHARED READING

A technique used generally in primary grades but adaptable to any grade where new language patterns are introduced.

The shared reading experience consists of a model reader reading aloud while others join in. In primary grades "big books", those with print large enough to be seen at a distance, are often used. Overhead transparencies also work well.

The model reader should read slowly enough so that children can follow the line of print as the reader's hand moves along the line. Model reading includes pausing at appropriate points in the text and using the rise or fall of the voice appropriately.

Shared reading materials can include the text of a story, poetry, song lyrics, chants or any other material.

Techniques for shared reading include:

REPETITION: Sharing the story or poem many times.

PATTERNING: Selecting stories or poems with repeating patterns.

ECHO READING: Reading a line from a poem and having children repeat or echo the line.

TRACKING: Moving the hand or finger along the line being read as children listen to establish the connection between what they are seeing and what they are hearing.

FADING: As children grow confident in their ability to read the text the model reader gradually softens his/her voice and stops reading while the young readers continue.

Shared reading is equally appropriate for older students through senior high school when they meet new language patterns. Shakespeare, for example, must be read aloud and modeled before students can read with meaning.

TO BEGIN: Choose books with repeating patterns. Here are a few favorites.

Allen, Pamela. BERTIE AND THE BEAR. Coward-McCann, 1985.

Fox, Mem. HATTIE AND THE FOX. Bradbury, 1986.

Kovalski, Maryann. WHEELS ON THE BUS. Little Brown, 1988.

Lobel, Anita. THE ROSE IN MY GARDEN. Harper & Row, 1984.

Martin, Bill Jr. BROWN BEAR, BROWN BEAR, WHAT DO YOU SEE? Holt, 1983.

Polette, Nancy. THE LITTLE OLD WOMAN AND THE HUNGRY CAT. Greenwillow, 1989.

Robart, Rose. THE CAKE THAT MACK ATE. Little Brown, 1988.

SHARED READING: POETRY 🔳9

Shared reading: Nine ways to share poems.

1. Read it aloud.

2. Read a line and have students echo the line back to you.

3. Divide the class into two groups. Groups read aloud alternate lines.

4. Underline key words, write to the side of each line and create a much shorter version of the poem.

5. Elaborate: what words, phrases can be added after each line for students to say and demonstrate.

6. Make an overhead transparency of the poem. Teacher and students read it aloud together (shared reading).

7. Read the poem to rhythm music. Read aloud with soft mood music in the background.

8. Try singing the Dickinson poem to the tune of "The Yellow Rose of Texas."

9. Add new verses.

THE ELF AND THE DORMOUSE

Under a toadstool crept a wee elf,
Out of the rain to
shelter himself.
Under the toadstool, all in a heap,
Was a dormouse, fast asleep.

"I can't stay here," said the elf, and yet,
"If I leave I'll get all wet."
The next shelter was far,
Almost a mile.
Then the wee elf smiled a wee smile.

Tugged at a toadstool broke it in two.
Up over his head and away he flew.
Soon reached home, dry as can be.
The dormouse woke up and said,
"Good gracious me!"

My toadstool is missing,"
he loudly lamented.
And that's how umbrellas
First were invented.

                                    Oliver Herford

Try using some of the above sharing ideas with this poem entitled "March" by Emily Dickinson.

Dear March—Come in—
How glad I am—
I hoped for you before—
Put down your Hat—
You must have walked—
How out of Breath you are—
Dear March, how are you, and the Rest—
Did you leave Nature well—
Oh March, Come right up stairs with me—
I have so much to tell—

PREDICTIVE READING 🔟

Read the following story aloud or make a transparency and read together with students. Uncover only that portion of the transparency you are reading. Stop at appropriate points and ask for predictions. Check to see if the student has a reason for the prediction.

The Contented Old Woman

One day a poor old woman was digging potatoes in her garden. All at once she stooped and pulled out of the earth a big iron pot full of gold. She was pleased as she could be.

She dragged it a little way toward her house, and looked again to make sure that it was full of gold. What do you think she found?

The gold had turned into silver! She was as pleased as she could be. She dragged it a little further and had to stop for breath. She looked again to make sure it was full of silver. What do you suppose had happened?

The silver had turned to copper pennies. Still she was as pleased as she could be. At the door she looked again to make sure that she had her pennies safe. Well, what do you think she saw?

There was nothing in the pot but a heavy stone. She remembered that she needed just such a stone to keep her door open. She was still as pleased as she could be. As she stooped to pick up the stone, what do you suppose happened?

The stone turned into a hideous dragon breathing fire. He jumped over her flower beds and flew away. Do you think the old woman was cross then?

No, she clapped her hands and cried, "Oh, how lucky I am! He might have eaten me up, house and garden and all!" So the contented old woman baked potatoes for supper and went to sleep in her cozy bed.

PREDICTIVE READING 🔟

Predictive questions to ask

Ask about what *will* be read, not what has been read.

1. What does the title mean?

2. What will the story be about?

3. What is the problem?

4. What will happen next?

5. Why do you predict that?

6. What are other possibilities?

7. Given what you know, what do you think will be the outcome?

8. How can we find out?

9. When were you sure?

10. What is this story really about (theme)?

PARTNERSHIP READING ▥

What the Teacher Does

1. Demonstrate the predictive reading lesson with the class showing students how to use questions that predict action.

2. Assign reading partners. (partners do not have to have the same reading level)

3. Assign individual reading selections based on student interest and ability. (can be self-selected if appropriate to the reading level of the student)

4. Independent reading time. Teacher calls stop after 3-5 minutes.

5. Each student writes one question that has arisen and a possible answer, or tells the reading partner what has happened in the story and what question needs to be answered now.

6. Continue independent reading. At the conclusion of the reading, students share with partners: (see note below)
   A. Story summary.
   B. What they thought would happen.
   C. What did happen.

7. Oral reading. Each student reads aloud a favorite page to his/her partner.

8. Students volunteer to read aloud to the class a favorite paragraph.

NOTE: If one partner completes the reading well before the other, ask the speedy reader to look back through the text of his/her selection to find sentences (and be prepared later in the lesson to read them aloud) that contain examples of any skills you want to review. Example: Find a sentence that contains at least five of the following: a proper noun, a common noun, a collective noun, a word with a prefix, a word with a suffix, a contraction, a possessive noun, an adverb that tells how, an adverb that tells when, a homonym, an example of alliteration, a metaphor, a simile.

READERS THEATRE

A suitable strategy for all grades 1-8.
Scripts selected or written are suited to the maturity level of the students.

Benefits
1. Practice in oral interpretation
2. Greater understanding of literary elements
3. Develops empathy with a character...allows the child to walk in another's shoes
4. Allows for search for meaning beyond the printed word
5. All children can participate
6. Does **not** require extensive props or scenes
7. Students adapt and write their own scripts

Tips for Effective Readers Theatre
1. Use a narrator to set the scene and to move the action.
2. Readers remain in one position.
3. Readers can turn away, fold scripts or look down when the action moves away from them.
4. Props are kept to a minimum. Hats, collars, or small signs can be helpful.
5. No props are held in the reader's hands. All attention should be on the reading.
6. Select literature worth the time of the children in adapting and reading the script.
7. A good literature selection should leave children with as many questions as answers.
8. Adapt entire picture books or short stories. From novels adapt scenes that will stand alone and at the same time challenge the audience to want to read the novel.

Script Adaptation Requires
1. Selecting the important from the unimportant.
2. Ability to move action from one scene to another without leaving "gaps."
3. Practice in changing narration to dialogue.
4. Understanding of character, plot, setting, mood and theme to select those elements which best display these literature components.

Readers Theatre **can** make a significant contribution to the reading and literature program of your class! Good oral interpretation is a **product** of hard work, thorough comprehension and deep understanding of the point of view of another.

Teachers of ESL students and of reading disabled students often report that their students will read parts in a Readers Theatre script with greater facility than reading aloud any other material. Taking on another role frees them from the fear of making mistakes.

READERS THEATRE SCRIPT 🎬
To Catch A Bear

Adapted from an old Russian tale.

Reading parts: (1) Old Woman (2) Bear (Bruin) (3) Narrator

NARRATOR: Once there was an old woman who was walking in the forest when she spied a cherry tree. She climbed up the tree to gather wild cherries when a bear happened by.

BRUIN: Come down, old woman. Come down at once for I have not yet had breakfast and I want to eat you.

OLD WOMAN: Eat me indeed! Why would any self respecting bear want to eat a scrawny old woman like me? Here, gnaw on my shoe while I pick these cherries. Then I will take you to my house. I have two plump children who are just the right size for a bear's breakfast. So wait a bit until I can serve them up to you.

NARRATOR: The old woman threw down one of her shoes. The bear chewed and chewed upon it but the more he chewed, the hungrier he got.

BRUIN: Come down at once! I can wait no longer. Did you not ever hear the expression, "Hungry as a bear." Well, I am!

OLD WOMAN: Just a bit longer while I get the cherries at the top of the tree. Here, chew on my other shoe. I'll soon come down and show you the way to my house.

NARRATOR: The bear chewed and chewed but was still hungry. Finally the old woman came down and led the way home with the bear tramping behind her.

OLD WOMAN: Here we are home just as I said. I'll tell you what. First let me give the children a good meal so that I can fatten them up for you. Meanwhile, run about the forest until mid day to get up a better appetite.

BEAR: Hmmmm, I suppose two juicy children would taste better than one old woman. I'll wait until you fatten them up, but I will be back at mid day.

NARRATOR: Meanwhile the old woman looked about the cottage for anything she could use to get rid of that bear. She saw the frog her children had caught. It was hiding in a bucket. The pigeon in the rafters was staying as far away as it could from the cat. She saw the cuckoo clock on the wall, matches by the stove, a balloon, an old saw, a teakettle, a candle, an umbrella, a rope and a horn and a fifty pound bag of potatoes.

READERS THEATRE SCRIPT 🔢
To Catch A Bear (continued)

OLD WOMAN: There must be some way to get rid of that bear. He will be so hungry by mid day that he will surely break down my door. I must be ready for him. What can I do?

NARRATOR: How can you combine any five of the items the old woman has to get rid of the bear. One must act on the next one which will act on the next one and so on to achieve the desired result, that is, to remove the hungry bear as a danger to the old woman and her children.

Write your ideas here:

_____

_____

_____

_____

_____

_____

_____

_____

_____

BRUIN: Here I am, old woman. Now bring out your children and let me eat them up for I am starving to death.

OLD WOMAN: Did you think I would really give you my children? Foolish bear. Go away. I shall not unbar the door.

BRUIN: Then I shall break it in. Here I come. And once inside I will eat you as well.

NARRATOR: The bear gave a great leap and broke open the door ...

AUDIENCE: Share your endings for the story. Tell how combining five of the items the old woman had available will do away with the bear.

The End

Critical listening involves drawing conclusions or making decisions or judgements based on what is heard. The listener must *analyze* what is presented. The EYEWITNESS report below requires analysis to *decide* who is telling the truth. Assign reading parts. Tell the class that they will have to vote on who the real eyewitness is after hearing the play. The script contains obvious clues for the good listener! This script can also be duplicated and used as a writing model for students' own reporting of an historical incident.

LARRY OR LORETTA BORE:
Welcome everyone to our show, EYEWITNESS. Only one eyewitness is telling the complete truth. It is up to you to guess which it is. Now let's meet our guests. Eyewitness #1, what is your name?

EYEWITNESS #1: My name is Jemima Boone and I was an eyewitness to the siege of Boonesborough, Sept. 7, 1778.

BORE: Eyewitness #2, what is your name?

EYEWITNESS #2: My name is Jemima Boone. I was an eyewitness to the siege of Boonesborough on Sept. 7, 1777, along with my husband, Daniel.

BORE: Eyewitness #3, what is your name?

EYEWITNESS #3: My name is Jemima Boone, wife of Daniel Boone and I was an eyewitness to the siege of Boonesborough on Sept. 7, 1778.

BORE: Eyewitness #1, tell us your story.

EYEWITNESS #1: We only had about 50 men and boys to protect us against 400 braves led by Chief Black Fish. It was a fearsome sight...then Black Fish asked for a parley. Alone and unarmed, Daniel Boone went out to meet them.

BORE: Eyewitness #2, then what happened?

EYEWITNESS #2: Somehow a peace treaty was hammered out, but before it could be signed, the Indians grabbed father, but he threw Blackfish to the ground and was shot in the shoulder getting back to the fort.

BORE: Eyewitness #3, is that when the attack started?

EYEWITNESS #3: Yes, the Indians cut the telegraph wires, then they massed for a charge on the North wall. The women and children were hidden away in case the Indians broke through.

EYEWITNESS #1: They were not! We *all* grabbed spare rifles and manned the loopholes. We wanted the Indians to think there were twice as many of us as there were.

EYEWITNESS #2: Then the fire arrows started and flames licked through the fort. Dazed, we fell back to the blockhouse and passed buckets of water from the well.

EYEWITNESS #3: If that weren't bad enough, the Indians began digging a tunnel to lay powder charges under the fort. But during the night the rains came and at dawn the tunnels had collapsed. The Indians tried one more morning assault but we held them off and they gave up and left.

BORE: Now it is time to decide who is the real eyewitness to the siege of Boonesborough. We will vote by a show of hands. Is it #1? (Wait for show of hands) Is it #2? (Wait for show of hands) Is it #3? (Wait for show of hands)

Now for the moment you have all been waiting for. Will the real Jemima Boone, eyewitness to the siege of Boonesborough, please step forward.

For exciting reading about this siege and other events in the life of Daniel Boone read:
Daniel Boone: Frontier Adventures by Keith Brandt. Troll, 1983
Daniel Boone: Pioneer Trailblazer by Jim Hargrove. Children's Press 1985
Daniel Boone: Young Hunter and Tracker by Augusta Stevenson. Macmillan 1983

Answer: The real Jemina Boone is #1. #2 states at one point that she is the wife of Daniel Boone and at another that she is his daughter. #3 refers to the cutting of the telegraph wires. The telegraph had not been invented in the 1700's.

QUESTIONS TO ASK AFTER READING
(all grade levels)

How many ways ...

What if ...

Suppose that ...

If you were ...

How is ... like ...

LITERATURE QUESTIONING TECHNIQUES

For Upper Elementary/Middle School and Junior High Students

OBJECTIVE: By using the questions that follow with *any* literature selection, the teacher should see a deepening of the levels of response and a growing awareness on the part of students that literature is a way by which one can experience life and commonality among all mankind.

1. Not all questions need to be asked. Use those most appropriate to the literature selection.

2. After students have been guided through the questioning process by the teacher, literature discussion groups can be formed for other selections. Students can use these questions as a guide in their self-directed group discussions.

Four Levels Of Questions

Objective
1. What words or phrases do you remember?
2. What people do you remember seeing?
3. What colors, objects, sounds, textures do you recall?

Reflective
4. Whom did you like or dislike in the story?
5. With whom did you identify ?
6. What emotions did you see in the story? When?
7. What kind of music would you choose to accompany this story?

Interpretative
8. Was there any point in the story when you felt happy? sad? apprehensive? angry? disappointed?
9. If you could have stopped the story at any point, where would you have stopped it?
10. If you needed to shorten the story where would you have made the cuts?

Decisional
11. How do you think the main character felt at the end of the story?
12. Have you ever felt like this?
13. Who needs to read this story? (Think of an historical figure or another character from literature).
14. If you could be any of the characters, which would you choose to be?
15. What title would you give this story?

ASKING QUESTIONS
TO COMPARE TALES!!!

Think of a question that each of these literary characters might ask the other. Your question needs to be related in some way to the characters or the stories.

1. What directions might Prince Charming ask of Rapunzel?

2. What question might Jack and the Beanstalk ask of Paul Bunyan?

3. What would Cinderella ask to borrow from Rumplestiltskin?

4. What question might Snow White ask Sleeping Beauty?

5. If Henny Penny passed by the troll under the bridge in The Three Billy Goats Gruff, what would she ask?

6. What question would the wolf in Red Riding Hood have for the wolf in the Three Little Pigs?

7. What question might the witch in Snow White ask the witch in the gingerbread house in Hansel and Gretel?

8. What question might Tom Thumb have for the giant in Jack and the Beanstalk?

9. What question might the Twelve Dancing Princesses ask the shoemaker from The Elves and the Shoemaker?

10. What would Goldilocks ask to borrow from Little Red Riding Hood? Why?

COMPARING TALES 18

After reading _____ and _____, complete the
information in the boxes below

Main character		
Other characters		
Setting		
Main problem		
How was the problem solved?		

How are the stories alike? _____

_____

_____

How are the stories different? _____

_____

_____

Which story did you like best? _____

_____

KEEP A WORD BANK BOOK
Grades 1-3

Each page in your word bank book will have words that are alike in some way.

Describing words
beautiful
ugly
large
handsome
wicked
warty
little

Name Words
(Fairy tale characters)
queen
princess
prince
dragon
toad
troll
witch

Action words
sits
stands
hops
hides
skips
sings
cries

Words that tell where
in the kitchen
under the hill
above the mountain
on the chair
into the water
between the pages
on the lilypad

Use words from your word bank pages to write sentences about a character from a fairy tale you have read.

Example: A warty toad hops into the water.

A large dragon hides under the hill.

A beautiful queen sits on the chair.

Write your sentences here:

_____

_____

_____

_____

WRITING SONGS TO CHECK STORY COMPREHENSION AND TO TEACH SENTENCE STRUCTURE Grades 1-3

Summarizing James Marshall's <u>Red Riding Hood.</u>

Pattern for: Are You Sleeping?

<u>BIG</u>	<u>BAD</u>	<u>WOLF</u>
adjective	adjective	name of a character

<u>BIG</u>	<u>BAD</u>	<u>WOLF</u>
adjective	adjective	name of a character

<u>IN THE WOODS</u>
prepositional phrase telling where the character was

<u>AT GRANDMA'S HOUSE</u>
prepositional phrase telling where the character was

<u>WAITING</u>	and	<u>TALKING</u>
ing verb		ing verb

<u>POUNCING</u>	and	<u>EATING</u>
ing verb		ing verb

<u>HUNTER CAME</u>
three syllable word or phrase to end the story

<u>GRANDMA SAVED</u>
another three syllable word or phrase or repeat three syllable word or phrase above

Pattern for: Skip to My Lou

<u>LITTLE</u>	<u>GIRL</u>	<u>WALKING</u>	<u>IN THE WOODS</u>
adjective	noun	verb	prepositional phrase

<u>HUNGRY</u>	<u>WOLF</u>	<u>HIDING</u>	<u>BEHIND THE TREE</u>
adjective	noun	verb	prepositional phrase

<u>WHITE-HAIRED</u>	<u>GRANDMA</u>	<u>READING</u>	<u>IN THE BED</u>
adjective	noun	verb	prepositional phrase

<u>WHAT DO YOU THINK WILL HAPPEN?</u>
seven syllable last line (any part of speech)

WRITING SONGS TO CHECK STORY COMPREHENSION AND TO TEACH SENTENCE STRUCTURE [20]

Pattern for: Are You Sleeping?

_____   _____   _____
adjective   adjective   name of a character

_____   _____   _____
adjective   adjective   name of a character

_____
prepositional phrase telling where the character was

_____
prepositional phrase telling where the character was

_____ and _____
ing verb   ing verb

_____ and _____
ing verb   ing verb

_____
three syllable word or phrase to end the story

_____
another three syllable word or phrase or repeat three syllable word or phrase above

Pattern for: Skip to My Lou

_____   _____   _____   _____
adjective   noun   verb   prepositional phrase

_____   _____   _____   _____
adjective   noun   verb   prepositional phrase

_____   _____   _____   _____
adjective   noun   verb   prepositional phrase

_____
seven syllable last line (any part of speech)

RESPONDING TO LITERATURE IN SONG

Grades 2-4

Older students enjoy summarizing stories in song for younger students to sing. "My Bonnie Lies Over the Ocean" is an easy song pattern to use.

After sharing <u>Rumplestiltskin</u> illustrated by Paul Galdone (Clarion Books, 1985), ask students to sing this song and fill in the missing words using context clues.

RUMPLESTILTSKIN

A poor man arrived at the palace
And entered the throne room so bold,
He told the king, "My lovely (1) d_____
Can spin plain old (2) s_____ into (3) g_____

Chorus:
Oh dear! What now?
The poor maiden shivered with cold and dread,
Spin straw to (4) g _____
Or risk losing her pretty (5) h _____.

She met a man named (6) R _____
And made him a promise so wild,
The (7) s _____ turned to gold just like magic
"I'll be back," he said, "For your (8) c _____."

Chorus:
Oh dear! What now?
The poor (9) m _____ shivered with cold and dread,
Give up her (10) c _____?
She just did not mean what she said.

The (11) k _____ and the maiden were (12) m _____
And they had a beautiful child,
The little man showed up to claim him,
She guessed his (13) n _____ and he went (14) w _____

Chorus:
Oh, dear! What now?
In anger the little man turned around
He stomped so hard
That he fell right into the (15) g _____.

Answers: 1. daughter 2. straw 3. gold 4. gold 5. head 6. Rumplestiltskin 7. straw 8. child 9. maiden 10. child 11. king 12. married 13. name 14. wild 15. ground

54

VOCABULARY GAMES
Using illustrations from ABC books to build vocabulary power. (All grades)

Select an ABC book that has a number of items beginning with the same letter on each page. Make an overhead transparency of one illustration or use the book in a small group so that everyone can see the illustration *or* clip the book open and leave it in an accessible place so that students can look at it as time permits. Challenge individual students or teams of students to one or more of the writing response activities below. Announce the time limit for the contest. For example, if individual students are competing they may have all day to work on the activity in their spare time. Entries can be handed in at the end of the day and a winner announced the next morning.

Word Game Activities

1. In five minutes list all the **A** words you find. Look for nouns, verbs, and adjectives.

2. Which team can write the longest alliterative sentence based on what you see in the picture? All words in the sentence must begin with the letter **A**, except the words A, AN, THE, ON, BY, OVER and AT. (Five minute time limit.)

3. Which team can write the most sentences describing something in the picture? Each sentence must contain a different preposition. (Five minute time limit.)

SKILLS FROM THE TEXT 🔲

In a literature-based approach to reading, the skills are always introduced and taught within the meaningful context of the literature selection.

Example one: Phonics

Who can find and read aloud a sentence in the story that has a word with the short **a** sound as in <u>a</u>nd or th<u>a</u>t.

Who can find and read aloud a sentence that has a word with a long **a** followed by a consonant and a final silent **e**?

Choose the phonics skills you want to emphasize. Be sure to ask students to read the sentence and then identify the specific word that contains the letter sound(s) you want to stress.

Example two: Kinds of Sentences

After reviewing the four kinds of sentences, challenge students working either individually or in groups to find one of each kind in the reading selection, read it aloud and identify it by type: declarative, imperative, interrogative, exclamatory.

Example three: Playing with sentences

Take a sentence from the story and expand it.

EXAMPLE: The |girls ran through the|forest |.
        |frightened |dark | all night long.
        |anxious |gloomy | that surrounded them.

Take several sentences from the story and combine them.

EXAMPLE: The girls ran.
             They ran through the forest.
             They ran to the king's house.
             The girls ran to the king's house in the forest.

Take a sentence from the story and rearrange it.

EXAMPLE: Molly ran and ran with the giant at her heels.
                 With the giant at her heels, Molly ran and ran.

Take a sentence from the story and give it new meaning by substituting words.

EXAMPLE:
My| neck will|stay where it belongs for you can never|cross the|bridge.
|head |sit |hit |table
|purse |wander |love |cat.

Example four: Descriptive words

Make a word bank of descriptive words used in the story *or* make a word bank for your future writing of descriptive words you think of as you look at one of the illustrations from the story. Look for words that tell how things *look, sound, feel, taste, smell.*

SKILLS FROM THE TEXT 🎴
(grades 3-6)

NOUNS

Nouns can be common, proper, singular, plural, possessive or collective.

From the book or story you are reading find and read aloud the following sentences:

Find a sentence that contains:

1. Both a common noun and a proper noun.

2. A singular noun which has been made plural by adding s.

3. A singular noun which has been made plural by adding es.

4. A singular possessive noun.

5. A plural possessive noun.

Write a sentence describing a character from the book you are reading. This sentence must contain a singular common noun, a plural common noun, a proper noun, a possessive noun, two adjectives and a verb.

PREFIXES AND SUFFIXES

A PREFIX is letters added to the beginning of a word to change the meaning
   an, de, dis, il, in, non, and un mean *not*
   after, ante, pre and pro mean *when*
   on, off, under, pro and sub mean *where*

A SUFFIX is letters added to the end of a word.
   Some suffixes added to nouns are ant, ent, er, ess, or, cy, ism
   Some suffixes added to adjectives are ful, ous, less, er, est, ble
   Some suffixes added to adverbs are ily, ly, ways, ise
   Some suffixes added to verbs are ed, ing, en, fy

From the selection you are reading find and read aloud a sentence that contains words with both a prefix and a suffix. Find and read aloud sentences from the story which contain words with any prefix or suffix listed in the box above.

SKILLS FROM THE TEXT 🔲

Phonics from Mother Goose

Name a person, place or thing from a Mother Goose rhyme that has:

A long **A** sound

A long **I** sound

A long **E** sound

A long **O** sound

A hard **G** sound

A soft **G** sound

A hard **C** sound

A soft **C** sound

Name a person, place or thing that contains one of these blends:

bl	br	cl	pr	sc	sk	tw	wr
cr	dr	dw	fl	fr	gl	gr	pl
sl	sm	sn	sp	st	sw	tr	scr
shr	spl	spr	squ	str	thr		

Name a person, place or thing from a Mother Goose rhyme that has:

a short **A, E, I, O** or **U**.

SKILLS FROM ILLUSTRATIONS

Look carefully at this illustration. How many **P** words can you think of that tell what you see?

Name words   Describing words   Action words   Place words

———————   ———————   ———————   ———————

———————   ———————   ———————   ———————

———————   ———————   ———————   ———————

Write a sentence that tells about the picture. Use as many words that begin with the letter **P** as you can.

———————————————————————————————————

———————————————————————————————————

———————————————————————————————————

SKILLS FROM THE TEXT
PARTS OF SPEECH
(grades 4-8)

From the story you are reading, find and be prepared to read aloud the following sentences:

1. A sentence that contains an adverb that tells how.

2. A sentence that contains an adverb that describes an adjective.

3. A sentence that contains three or more adjectives.

4. A sentence in which several adjectives are used to describe a character.

5. A sentence in which adjectives are used to describe a place.

6. A sentence that contains an irregular verb.

7. A sentence that contains a linking verb.

8. A sentence that contains an appositive.

SKILLS FROM THE TEXT
(grades 4-8)

From the story you are reading, find and read aloud the following:

1. A declarative sentence
2. An imperative sentence
3. An interrogative sentence
4. An exclamatory sentence
5. The subject of a sentence
6. The predicate of a sentence
7. A sentence with a direct object
8. A sentence with an appositive
9. A sentence with at least two pronouns
10. A sentence that contains a simile
11. A sentence with a homophone
12. A sentence with a homograph
13. A sentence that creates a word picture
14. A sentence that contains one or more contractions

SKILLS FROM THE TEXT

Be a word detective.

Find and read aloud sentences in the story which contain:

1. A common noun
2. A proper noun
3. A singular noun
4. A plural noun
5. A possessive noun
6. A linking verb
7. An irregular verb
8. A past tense verb
9. An adjective
10. Two adjectives together
11. An adverb that tells how
12. An adverb that tells where
13. A prepositional phrase
14. One sentence that contains at least five of the above!

SKILLS FROM THE TEXT 22

(grades 4-8)
CAPITALIZATION/PUNCTUATION

se capital letters: for proper names and as the first word in a sentence.
se a period at the end of a sentence and after abbreviations.
se commas: to separate words in a series; to separate two or more adjectives before a noun;
   before conjunctions when they join independent clauses; to set off appositives or direct
   address; to separate items in dates and addresses; after the greeting in a friendly letter and
   the closing in any letter.
se quotation marks before and after direct speech. Example: "You are invited," Mary said.
se apostrophes in contractions (combining two words into one). Example: do not / don't
irections: Make story strips for any story similar to those shown below. Give sets of strips (each
·t in random order) to small groups of students who work together to sequence the story and to
ld capitalization and punctuation. This is an excellent way for students to learn from each other.

benezer scrooge was a

reedy miser whose partner marley

as dead scrooge went home on christmas

ve and was visited by three ghosts

he first ghost took scrooge to the

ast the second took scrooge to the present

he third took him to the

uture where he saw his own grave

crooge decided to keep christmas after all

SKILLS FROM STORY ILLUSTRATIONS

(grades 3-6)

Look carefully at Paul Galdone's illustration of *The Steadfast Tin Soldier* by Hans Christian Andersen (Clarion 1979).

Make four columns on your paper. Label them:

Nouns	Verbs	Adjectives	Adverbs

List as many words as possible in each column based on what you see in the illustration.

Write a sentence describing the soldier which contains at least one word from each of your four lists.

Illustration from *The Steadfast Tin Soldier* by Hans Christian Andersen, Illustrated by Paul Galdone. Clarion Books, 1979. Included with permission.

SKILLS FROM STORY ILLUSTRATIONS

(grades 4-7) 23

Teacher note: any illustration can be used.

Responding to illustrations:

Sentence Sense

Based on the picture, write:

An interrogative sentence

_____

_____

An imperative sentence:

_____

_____

An exclamatory sentence

_____

_____

A sentence which contains a proper noun, a possessive noun, a plural noun and a contraction.

_____

_____

A sentence with a direct object.

_____

_____

A sentence that contains two nouns, three adjectives, two words with prefixes and suffixes, one or more verbs and at least one prepositional phrase.

_____

_____

STORYBOARDS
(grades 3-8)

Using the storyboard is an excellent way to think out a story before you actually write it. In setting up the storyboard you can change cards and thus consider several possibilities before you decide exactly how you want the story to develop. When the board is complete you have really created an outline for the plot of your story. You are then ready to write.

1. On the storyboard below are ten spaces. Space one is the character/setting space. Decide on a character and a setting for Space one. Write these items in the space. Think about the characters. Who are they? Do they know each other? Are they related? Ages?

2. Cut apart the incident cards. These are the incidents that move the story along. Choose one you think will fit in space two. You may change the incident cards at any time.

3. Space three is the problem. Decide what the problem is in general terms. For example: One character wants to do something but the other(s) do not. Who wants to do what? Why don't the others want to do it?

4. Continue moving the story along by placing incident cards in the empty spaces. By the time you reach space ten you should have solved the problem in space three.

STORYBOARDS

Fill the blank spaces on the storyboard below with the incident cards. Be sure in developing the story that the problem (space 3) and solution (space 10) match!

Storyboard

1. Character/Setting Two men in a submarine.	6.
2.	7.
3. Problem One wants to surface, the other does not.	8. Climax The stingray grew larger!
4.	9.
5.	10. Solution It was turned off.

Incident Cards

A bargain is made	It rains	Someone walks away
Someone runs	An army approaches	There's a knock at the door
An invitation arrives	The order is given	An animal escapes
A bottle is found	The cloud covers the sun	A magic ring is found
The earth trembles	There is silence	The load was heavy
They travel together	The sun comes up	Someone smiles
Someone sings	It is caught	Someone screams
Footsteps are heard	A bird appears	The search begins
The fight begins	The noise gets louder	They can't find it
It is invisible	It drops	It is fixed

When the storyboard is completed you are ready to write your own story!

LITERARY TERMS: BE A SENTENCE FINDER!

Alliteration: Repeating beginning sounds (Peter Piper picked)

Hyperbole: Absurd exaggeration...doing something to excess (Davy Crockett killed a bear when he was only three.)

Imagery: Use of the senses in describing (taste, smell, touch, sight, hearing).

Metaphor: Comparing without the use of like or as (The sea was a cauldron).

Personification: Giving life to nonliving objects (Fingers of wind plucked the clothes).

Repetition: Repeating phrases for emphasis. (His right foot, his enormous right foot, lifted up and out).

Simile: Comparing using like or as. (As neat as a pin).

From the selection you are reading find:

A sentence that contains a simile.

_____

_____

A sentence that contains alliteration.

_____

_____

A sentence which contains hyperbole.

_____

_____

A sentence with good imagery.

_____

_____

A sentence that contains a metaphor.

_____

_____

A sentence that uses repetition for effect.

_____

_____

A sentence that shows personification.

_____

_____

LITERATURE AS A SPRINGBOARD TO ORAL LANGUAGE DEVELOPMENT

Read silently this short tale from German folk literature.

EVERYBODY HELPED

A man once ordered a new dressing-gown from his tailor. When it came home, he tried it on, and found to his disgust that it was six inches too long. He flung it down in a rage and went out into the street to walk himself into a good temper.

His wife thought that she could very soon make right what was wrong. She took her shears and cut off six inches, and hemmed the gown as neatly as before, as a pleasant surprise for her husband when he came home.

Then she went to market and on the way stopped next door, where her husband's mother lived, and told how annoyed her husband was at the mistake. But she had to hurry to get vegetables for dinner, so she did not stop to tell what she herself had done.

Her mother-in-law thought it a great pity that such a mistake should not be corrected at once, so she went over to her son's house, and cut six inches off the dressing-gown, and hemmed it up as neatly as before.

Meanwhile, the man had passed the tailor's shop and told him of his mistake. The tailor at once sent a boy home with his angry patron, to get the dressing-gown and have it made right. So the tailor cut off six inches and hemmed the gown up as neatly as before.

When the man came to try it on again, it did not reach even to his knees.

FROM THE GERMAN.

Follow the directions on the next page for turning this story into a play.

PERFORMING A PLAY WITHOUT A WRITTEN SCRIPT

If we tried to make the play exactly like the story, we should have three different places for the action: the man's house, his mother's house, and the tailor's shop. But on the stage we try to have as few changes of scene as possible. Let us change the story so that everything will happen in the man's house:

Scene 1.   The tailor's boy brings in the dressing-gown, and goes. The man tries it on, and goes out in a rage.

Scene 2.   The wife cuts off the gown. The man's mother comes in, and is told the beginning of the story.

Scene 3.   The wife hurries off to market, without finishing the story. The mother cuts off the gown, and goes home.

Scene 4.   The man comes back with the tailor, who cuts it off again.

Scene 5.   The man's wife and mother come back while he is trying it on; and the whole story comes out.

Let the parts of the man, his wife, his mother, the tailor, and the tailor's boy be taken by five of the class; and let the others help decide what each player shall say and do.

RESPONDING TO LITERATURE WITH PATTERNS 26

Use the pattern below to describe two characters in the story you have read.
By adding additional verses you can tell about other characters in the story.

Example:

If I had the energy
of a Peter Pan
I would fly through the air
and I'd crow like a rooster
but I wouldn't sew shadows on
and act like a mother to lost boys
because only
Wendy does that

If I had the patience
of Wendy
I would care for lost boys
and sing them to sleep
but I wouldn't capture Peter Pan
or run from crocodiles
because only Captain Hook
does that.

Your turn

If I had the _____

of a _____

I would _____

And I'd _____

But I wouldn't _____

And _____

Because only _____

_____ do that!

PATTERNS 26
Reporting on a Story
with Three Characters

The pattern below combines how a character in a story felt and the action of other characters toward the main character. Here is an example of the pattern using *The Fisherman and His Wife*.

The fisherman's wife was greedy. She was so greedy that she sent him back to ask for things again and again. The fisherman knew that his wife felt greedy because she was never satisfied with the gifts he bought her. The magic fish knew that the wife felt greedy because he finally refused to answer any of her requests.

_____ was _____ .
character   feeling

He/she was so _____ that he/she
                                    feeling

_____ .
                                    action

_____ knew that _____
another character   first character

felt _____ because _____

_____ .

_____ knew that _____
third character   first character

felt _____ because _____

_____ .

BOOK REPORTS 🔳26

The poetry patterns on this page are all used to describe a character or scene from *The Wizard of Oz*. Choose a scene or character from this or another favorite tale and use one of the patterns below to tell about it.

Five Senses Poem

Color	The Emerald City is green.
Sound	It sounds like tinkling glass.
Taste	It tastes like lime popsicles.
Smell	It smells like Mr. Clean.
Sight	It looks like sparkling jewels.
Feeling	It makes me feel like dancing.

Phone Number Poem

Each line has the number of syllables in a chosen phone number.

3	Wicked Witch
3	Wanted shoes
4	Had to get them
8	Away from the girl who had them
6	Tried every way she could
6	Was defeated often
6	Wickedness does not pay!

Adverb Poem

1	Adverb	Firmly
2	Adverb	Surely
3	Adverb	Emphatically
4	Noun	Dorothy
5	Verb	Told
6	Noun with description	The Wicked Witch
7	Any word	NO!

Build A Name Poem

S	o wanted a brain
C	onfused
A	nd
R	attled until
E	veryone
C	onvinced him that his
R	esolve to
O	vercome danger proved his
W	isdom.

Bio Poem

Line		
1	First name	Wizard
2	Four traits	Talkative, charlatan, human, humbug
3	Related to	the people of Earth
4	Cares deeply about	returning to Earth
5	Who feels	embarrassed when discovered
6	Who needs	friends
7	Who gives	a chance to Dorothy
8	Who fears	the Wicked Witch of the West
9	Who would like to see	Oz free from danger
10	Resident of	the United States of America

BOOK REPORTS 🔲

The poetry patterns on this page are all used to describe a character or scene from
_____. Choose a scene or character from this or another
favorite tale and use one of the patterns below to tell about it.

Five Senses Poem

Color

Sound

Taste

Smell

Sight

Feeling

Build A Name Poem

Phone Number Poem

Each line has the number of syllables in
a chosen phone number.

Bio Poem

Line	
1	First name
2	Four traits
3	Related to
4	Cares deeply about
5	Who feels
6	Who needs
7	Who gives
8	Who fears
9	Who would like to see
10	Resident of

Adverb Poem

Adverb
Adverb
Adverb
Noun
Verb
Noun with
description
Any word

A MODEL FOR DESCRIBING REAL OR LITERARY PLACES

A Five Senses Report

Color:

Looks like:

Sounds like:

Smells like:

Tastes like:

It makes me feel like:

A Circus
A circus is many bright colors.
It looks like a patchwork quilt.
It sounds like six record players
going all at once.
It smells like sawdust.
It tastes like cotton candy.
It makes me feel like laughing.

Select a real place or the setting of a favorite tale to write about.

Example: The Alaskan Tundra from *Julie of the Wolves* or the chocolate factory from *Charlie and the Chocolate Factory.*

Write your report.

_____
title

Color: _____

Looks like: _____

Sounds like: _____

Smells like: _____

Tastes like: _____

It makes me feel like: _____

_____

Write and illustrate a guidebook
Consider:
    A guidebook to a real place like your school
    A guidebook to a literary place like the Land of Oz
    An Explorer's Guide to Our Town
    An Explorer's Guide to the Local Shopping Center

Choose one of the topics above or select your own topic.

Be sure to tell:
1. Where the reader is going, what special clothing or equipment he or she will need, and how long the trip will be.
2. What sights, sounds, smells are present at the site.
3. If people are present at the site, tell their jobs.
4. Use plenty of illustrations. These can be photographs, pictures cut from old magazines or your own illustrations. Think of a good caption for each illustration.

A RESEARCH REPORTING MODEL
Fact or Fiction?

FACT OR FICTION?

Louis Pasteur was an "A" student in science.

In using this model you will create a book. On one page you will make a statement and ask your reader if the statement is fact or fiction. On the next page you will tell your reader the answer and provide details showing why the statement is fact or fiction.

Topics for your book can range from the life of one person (real or literary) to a fact or fiction book about a place or event in history. Fact and fiction books can also be written about things (e.g.. stars).

FICTION !

Pasteur was considered by most of his teachers to be a below average student. His slowness to answer when questioned irritated those who taught him. His father noticed, however, that while he took a long time to think about a problem that when he did figure it out he was usually right. This methodical mind was later in life to discover methods of vaccination for smallpox and pasteurization of milk.

GOOD QUEEN BESS

The Story of Elizabeth I of England
by Diane Stanley and Peter Vennema
Four Winds Press 1990

Good Queen Bess tells the story of Elizabeth I of England—a queen whose strong will, shrewd diplomacy, religious tolerance, and great love for her subjects won the hearts of her people and the admiration of her enemies.

The daughter of King Henry VIII, whose break with the Catholic Church forced all of England to accept a new religion, Elizabeth learned caution as a young princess. And when she became queen at the age of twenty-five, she put her lessons into action. A highly intelligent woman, Elizabeth knew how to stall, change her mind, and play one side against another to get her own way—with foreign countries, her councillors, and even her many suitors. With these tactics, Good Queen Bess steered her country through troubled times to the glorious era of peace and security that would be called the Elizabethan Age.

Diane Stanley's exquisitely detailed paintings provide memorable scenes of Elizabeth and her times. Her forceful personality, colorful court, and devoted subjects come vividly to life, as do her powerful rivals. Here are Mary, Queen of Scots, who made intricate plots to take the English throne, and King Philip II of Spain, who sent an ill-fated armada of ships against England and prayed for their victory. This lively and beautifully illustrated biography is a wonderful portrait of the remarkable queen who loved her people so dearly and ruled them so well.

Poetry is always fun to write. Here are two different poetry models used to tell about Queen Elizabeth I of England.

SUMMARIZE AS AN ACROSTIC POEM

G rowing up a princess
O thers wanted her throne
O ne day at the age of twenty-five
D eclared
Q ueen of England
U nderestimated by many
E ver determined to rule with
E mpathy for her people
N o detail overlooked
B eloved by her subjects
E nvied by her rivals
S teered England on a course of
S ecurity and peace for 45 years

WRITE A LIMERICK

Good Bess was the Queen of her day,
For forty-five years she would stay,
On her throne she would smile
Ruled with wisdom and guile
Determined to have her own way.

BIOGRAPHY REPORT

Subject's name _____ (Can be a real or fictional person) _____

Complete this questionnaire as if you *were* the subject!

1. If the Pied Piper of Hamlin asked me for money to rid our town of rats, I would:

   A. give money gladly
   B. work on a committee to raise the money.

   C. tell him "the more rats the better."
   D. say it's not my problem.

2. My favorite books are:

   A. fantasy tales
   B. adventure tales

   C. factual information
   D. sports stories

3. I feel it is best in any situation:

   A. to plan for it
   B. to dream about it

   C. to wait and see what happens
   D. to take immediate action

4. If I have a problem I prefer:

   A. to solve it myself
   B. individual counseling

   C. group counseling
   D. to ignore it

5. I would choose for a pet:

   A. a dog
   B. a cat

   C. a snake
   D. an exotic bird

6. I am most efficient in:

   A. planning
   B. predicting from scientific data

   C. discerning the moods of others
   D. using intuition as my guide

7. I remember best:

   A. how to perform a motor skill
   B. names

   C. faces
   D. statistics

8. My best subject in school is/was:

   A. speech
   B. philosophy

   C. math
   D. reading

9. I show my feelings:

   A. not at all
   B. easily

   C. in poetry, art or drama
   D. only when absolutely necessary

MYSTERY PERSON BIOGRAPHY REPORT

Here is a fun way to report on the life of a famous person!

1. Read a biography.

2. List eighteen things you discovered about the person. Number from one to eighteen. Be sure to include one or two very easy clues.

3. Play the game with your classmates.

Directions: Each contestant selects three numbers (one at a time). The reader reads the clue for each number. After each clue, the contestant can make one guess as to who the mystery person is. If the contestant does not guess correctly after three clues, another contestant selects three clues and has three guesses. The game continues until six contestants have had a try at selecting clues and guessing or until the mystery person is discovered.

CLUE#

1. My appearance is considered strange by some.

2. I always travel on foot.

3. I perform a useful service.

4. I am a musical character.

5. Robert Browning made me famous.

6. I like bright colors.

7. I achieved fame in Germany.

8. I detest injustice and combat it with all my power.

9. I charge for my services.

10. The River Weser is important to my work.

11. I achieved fame on July 26, 1284.

12. It is possible that my legend grew out of the Children's Crusade of 1212.

13. I play a musical instrument.

14. After I had performed a useful service, payment was refused.

15. The town of Hamelin requested my services.

16. My hat always has a feather in it.

17. No one knows my real name.

18. Koppen Hill played an important part in the legend about me.

ONE MOMENT IN HISTORY
A Model for Reporting Research on Historical Events

ections: Use the script that follows as a model for reporting on one important day or time
istory with yourself as the central character or observer. The model can be used to
cribe any place or event by changing the setting, clothing, people, objects and actions. Be
e to include sounds, smells, and feelings as well as sights. The underlined portions of the
ipt are those that should be changed depending on the place or time you are describing.

The Day The Pirates Came To Town

One hazy May morning you walk slowly down
e school hallway and stop. On either side of a
or are fierce pirates...they are calling for you
enter. You walk through the door...the sign
ys Library. Then as if by magnetic force you
e drawn to a book...bright blue with another
rate on the cover. You open the book and
ter another world.

You look down at your homespun breeches,
ur copper buckled belt and new leather boots.
ou are a child of 1813.

You are hurrying down a muddy street in
ew Orleans...rushing along to the wharf with
erchants and planters. The Queen is in. There
ill be much to buy from Jean Lafitte and his
rate crew today.

You stop and your heart pounds as you see a
rge notice nailed to a tree. Governor Claiborne
offering a reward of $500.00 to anyone who
elivers the Pirate Lafitte to the Sheriff of New
rleans. Yet there he is on the wharf...bold as
rass.

The crowd parts as the Pirate Boss of
arataria strides up the street. His eyes are
ughing. The sun shines on his cocked hat and
olished boots and glints off the sword at his
de.

He is close now, very close. He tosses a gold
oubloon in the air and smiles as you catch it.
hen with a flick of the wrist he rips off the
overnor's notice and puts another of his own
its place which reads:

I, Boss of Barataria, offer a reward of
5,000.00 to anyone who delivers Governor
illiam Claiborne to me, Jean Lafitte.

A roaring cheer goes up. The noise surrounds
ou, lifts you and carries you back to your
brary chair. The world of 1813 fades and you
re once again a child of the 1990s. You smile
nd look down at the gold doubloon in your
and.

One _____ (morning/evening
_____
(describe the weather)
_____
(tell how it awakens you)
and awakens you. Sounds of _____
(what)
from _____
(where)
beckon you, "come out, come out."

You dress quickly, race down the stairs
and throw open the door. Outside
everything is different. You look down at
your clothing. You, too, are different.
You are a child of _____
(year)

Your _____
(describe your clothing)
_____
(tell how the clothing feels)
You hurry_____
(tell where you are going)
_____
You hear _____
You see _____
You smell _____
A feeling of _____ overcomes you.
You look up at _____
(what)
and catch your breath as you see _____
(who)
He/she _____
(describe this famous person)
and _____
(tell something the person does)
Everyone listens to his/her words "___
_____."
The people around _____
(tell how they react)
_____.

A great feeling of _____ overwhelms
you, lifts you up and carries you back to
the door of your home. You open the door
and step inside. The world of _____
(year)
fades to the past and you are once again
a child of the 1990s.

EYEWITNESS 🔲 27

Use this script as a model for reporting on an historical event. One witness is telling the truth. The other two witnesses give some correct and *incorrect* information. Challenge your classmates to listen carefully to determine who the real eyewitness is!

CHARACTERS:
Host: Larry or Loretta Bore
Three Eyewitnesses
Three Panelists

BORE: Welcome everyone to our Eyewitness show. Let me explain what is going to happen. We have three panelists who will try to guess which of our guests is telling the truth. Only one was a real eyewitness to the raid on Pearl Harbor on December 7, 1941. Now let's meet our guests.

Eyewitness #1, where were you on December 7, 1941.

EYEWITNESS #1:
I was in Pearl Harbor aboard the Carrier, Oklahoma.

BORE: Eyewitness #2, where were you on December 7, 1941?

EYEWITNESS #2:
I was aboard the Battleship Arizona in Pearl Harbor.

BORE: Eyewitness #3, where were you on December 7, 1941?

EYEWITNESS #3:
I was aboard the Battleship Nevada.

BORE: Now it's up to our panelists to discover the real eyewitness to this day in history. Let's begin with panelist #1.

PANELIST #1:
Eyewitness #1, why were all those ships in the harbor on this fateful day?

EYEWITNESS #1:
Pearl Harbor was the home base for the United States Pacific Fleet and there my ship the Missouri was based.

PANELIST #1:
Eyewitness #2, with tensions so great between the United States and Japan, why wasn't the Pacific Fleet ready in case of an attack?

EYEWITNESS #2:
Peace talks were going on in Washington and seemed to be going well. We didn't expect war.

PANELIST #1:
Eyewitness #3, what were you doing when the attack began?

EYEWITNESS #3:
I was a member of the ship's band. We were playing the Star Spangled Banner as the flag was hoisted on our ship.

BORE: Let's hear now from Panelist #2.

PANELIST #2:
Eyewitness #1. What happened when the enemy planes were first sighted?

EYEWITNESS #1:
We saw torpedo planes heading for our ship. We raced for the guns and started shooting them out of the sky.

PANELIST #2:
Eyewitness #2, tell us about your experiences.

EYEWITNESS
(continued)

EYEWITNESS #2:

We had to break a lock on the ammunition compartment to load our guns. Five bombs hit the ship before we could start to fire.

PANELIST #2:

Eyewitness #3, what did the band do when the attack began?

EYEWITNESS #3:

We dropped our instruments and dove for cover. You can't shoot down planes with a trombone. All of us on the Arizona knew that.

PANELIST #3:

Eyewitness #1, what happened to your ship?

EYEWITNESS #1:

Three torpedoes tore through us. Our ship burst into flames and then rolled over and floated sideways in the water.

PANELIST #3:

Eyewitness #2, what happened to your ship?

EYEWITNESS #2:

The bombs exploded our ammunition compartment. Our ship jumped clear out of the water and then sank taking over 1000 of my shipmates with her. It was a sight I'll never forget.

PANELIST #3:

Eyewitness #3, What happened to your ship?

EYEWITNESS #3:

Even though we were badly damaged the Captain ordered the ship out to sea. We were able to break through the harbor entrance on our way to find the enemy carriers and destroy them.

BORE: Our time is up for questions. Now it is time for the audience to vote by a show of hands.

Is it #1? (Wait for show of hands)
Is it #2? (Wait for show of hands)
Is it #3? (Wait for show of hands)

And now for the moment you have all been waiting for.

Will the real Eyewitness to the attack on Pearl Harbor on December 7, 1941 please step forward.

Note: To discover which statements are not precisely true, read *The Story of the U.S.S Arizona* by R. Conrad Stein. Children's Press, 1977.

PICK A PROJECT!
A Research Organizer (Grades 3-4)

Step One:	**Step Two:**	**Step Three:**
Choose and circle one action word	Choose and circle one topic	Choose and circle one product

Step One:
Choose and circle one action word

Label

List

Describe

Locate

Report

Show

Group

Discover

Compose

Create

Demonstrate

Choose

Tell About

Step Two:
Choose and circle one topic

Brainstorm with the class for topics to list here which are related to the literature selection you are reading or are related to a non-fiction research project.

List as many topics as you can.

Example:

If the topic listed here was "Heart Transplants" (what the Tinman wanted in the Wizard of Oz), I might decide to report on the first doctor to perform a heart transplant as a Bio-Poem or an Interview.

Step Three:
Choose and circle one product

Acrostic poem

Chart

Story

Model

Map

Mobile

Diorama

Bio-poem

Report

True/false book

Drawing

Write a sentence telling what you will do to report on the topic you choose. In your sentence include an action word and a product as well as your topic.

_____action_____   _____topic_____   _____product_____

_____

_____

PICK A PROJECT! 28
A Research Organizer (Grades 5-8)

<u>Step one:</u>
Choose and circle one action word

<u>Step two:</u>
Choose and circle one topic.

<u>Step three:</u>
Choose and circle one product.

ACTION
(Choose one)

TOPIC

PRODUCT
(Choose one)

<u>Knowledge</u>
Define
Record
Label
List

<u>Comprehension</u>
Summarize
Describe
Locate
Report

<u>Application</u>
Solve
Demonstrate
Dramatize
Show

<u>Analysis</u>
Compare
Categorize
Classify
Discover

<u>Synthesis</u>
Compose
Hypothesize
Predict
Create

<u>Evaluation</u>
Judge
Rank order
Criticize
Recommend

Brainstorm with the class as many topics as possible to write in this center section.

Topics should be related to the non-fiction study in a current subject area or can be topics related to a literature selection.

Acrostic poem
Advice letter
Autobiography
Bio-poem
Chart
Choral reading
Collage
Comic strip
Concert reading
Diorama
Editorial
Essay
Eyewitness report
Fable
Filmstrip
Interview
Journal
Lesson
Map
Model
Moment in history script
Mystery person report
Newspaper
Oral report
Poem
Question/answer session
Readers theatre script
Report
Song
Story
Tape recording
Time line
TV script
True/false book

ACTION	TOPIC	PRODUCT
Describe		as an acrostic poem

EVALUATION
Evaluation of written research products

	NO	YES
Use of a variety of sources	1	10
Contains factual information backed up by list of sources	1	10
Information clear and understandable	1	10
Neat and attractive	1	10
Correct spelling	1	10
Correct punctuation	1	10
Inclusion of details or elaborations	1	10
Use of interesting vocabulary	1	10
Correct grammar	1	10
Followed directions	1	10

Total possible points = 100 Your score _____

Evaluation of non-written research products

	NO	YES
Use of a variety of sources	1	10
Presents core material is a new manner	1	10
Attention to detail	1	10
Accompanied by a list of sources of information	1	10
Design: color arrangement, composition (how is the eye drawn?)	1	10
Neatness	1	10
Labels or lettering correctly spelled	1	10
Information clear and understandable	1	10
Logical connection between product and core material	1	10
Followed directions	1	10

Total possible points = 100 Your score _____

EVALUATION
Evaluation of original stories

	NO	YES
Shows a concept of plot (story has a beginning, middle and end)	1	10
Describes the setting	1	10
Describes the character(s)	1	10
Relates setting to plot	1	10
Shows logical sequence of action	1	10
Story problem is easily identified	1	10
Story solution makes sense	1	10
Use of interesting vocabulary	1	10
Correct grammar	1	10
Correct spelling/punctuation	1	10

Neatness shows pride in your work! Total possible points = 100 Your score _____

EVALUATION
Evaluation of individual pupil progress
Reporting to Parents

Periodic progress reports to parents indicate the progress the student is making in the various subject areas. As demonstrated below, each grade level progress report indicates those skills usually mastered by most students at that level. Reports are compiled through careful teacher observation of progress, portfolios of students' work and oral and written assessments.

Name: _____ Year: _____

Grade: _____ Teacher: _____ School: _____

SKILL	R	S	M*	COMMENTS	DATE
READING					
• Reads silently for a sustained period					
• Reads a variety of materials such as: poetry, stories, songs, informational					
• Demonstrates an understanding of text:					
- predicts outcomes and actions					
- retells story or information in own words					
- talks about characters					
- identifies main idea(s)					
- locates specific parts of text					
- describes setting					
- expresses reasons for liking or disliking a story					
- uses pictures to support the meaning of the story					
• Reads fluently with appropriate phrasing					
• When in difficulty, uses a variety of strategies successfully:					
- integrates context cues:					
. meaningful/picture cues					
. structure cues					
. visual/phonetic cues					
- reads on to end of sentence					
- starts sentence again and re-reads					
- self-corrects when errors interfere with meaning.					
WRITING					
• Writes on a regular basis					
• Writes on a variety of topics:					
- self initiated					
- teacher initiated					
• Writes a completed series of ideas in an organized manner					
• Chooses appropriate words to convey meaning					
• Keeps a collection of writings					
• Produces a published piece of writing:					
- revises and rewrites					
- edits					
. spells most familiar words correctly					
. uses end punctuation					
. uses appropriate capitalization					
• Demonstrates knowledge of the appropriate mechanics of writing					

KEY: R = rarely S = sometimes
    M = Most of the time; * denotes mastery

PART TWO

INTEGRATED THEMATIC UNITS

The units which follow integrate reading and language arts as well as numerous other subject disciplines:

For grades one, two and three:
   Animals of Africa

For grades four, five, six and seven:
   Books with a Dickensian flavor

For grades six, seven and eight:
   Ocean voyages

INTEGRATING LITERATURE STUDIES: PRIMARY GRADES—ANIMALS OF AFRICA by Nancy Polette © 1991

LANGUAGE ARTS

1. Make a dictionary of African animals following the pattern in Mary Elting's Q IS FOR DUCK (Houghton, 80). Example: T is for elephant! Why? The explanation follows.
2. Write an "If I had the feet of" pattern story about an African animal.
3. Select skills needed by students (example: parts of speech). Ask them to identify the skill in a sentence in the book(s) they are reading *or* write a sentence based on an illustration from the book which shows the student understands and can use the skill.
4. Write a paragraph about an African animal following the pattern in Margaret Wise Brown's THE IMPORTANT BOOK (Harper Trophy, 90). "The important thing about a lion is…." Do topic talking about topics related to a story *before* sharing the story.
5. Predict those animals that will be in the story and *listen* carefully to support or deny the predictions.

ART

Note the use of animal masks by the dancers in Aardema's WHO'S IN RABBIT'S HOUSE? Design and make animal masks to retell the story. Share Shirley Glubok's ART OF AFRICA, (Macmillan, 74) which contains several authentic masks.

PROBLEM SOLVING/CRITICAL THINKING

1. After sharing a list of African animals and discussing habitats, ask student to identify African animals in Graeme Base's ANAMALIA (Abrams, 86) and Simon's ANIMAL FACT/FABLE. (Crown, 79)
2. Share 1 HUNTER by Pat Hutchins (Mulberry 86). Which animal does *not* belong in the story? (tiger) Why? (No tigers in Africa).
3. Develop a problem solving grid for the problem faced by the main character in any story shared. Challenge students to list alternatives and criteria and to come up with a solution. Compare their solutions to the author's solution.

SOCIAL STUDIES/GEOGRAPHY

1. Locate Africa on a map. How many countries are in Africa? See: TRUE BOOK OF AFRICA by D. V. Georges (Child. 86)
2. Discuss the difference between a country and a continent.
3. Locate four major regions in Africa — grasslands, deserts, mountains, jungle. Which African animals live in which region? See: Aruego, Jose, WE HIDE, YOU SEEK (Greenwillow, 79)

MATH

Using animals in any story, make up story problems to solve. Example: If rabbit found twice as many creatures in his house, how many would there be?

TO INTRODUCE THE UNIT

THE VINGANANEE AND THE TREE TOAD by Verna Aardema and WHO IS COMING? by Patricia McKissack

RESEARCH PROJECTS

Choose one African animal. Read about the life and habits of the animal. Report on the animal as:

1. An acrostic poem
2. A true/false book. For a model see ANIMAL FACT, ANIMAL FABLE by Seymour Simon (Crown, 79).
3. A paragraph following the model in Brown's THE IMPORTANT BOOK. (Harper, 90)

MUSIC

1. Share the picture book version of the African lullaby, ABIYOYO by Pete Seeger. Sing the song (music is included). (Macmillan, 88)
2. Create songs based on the stories read.

SCIENCE

1. Name and group African animals. Try for as many groups as possible: mammals, reptiles, birds, by habitat, meat eaters, plant eaters and more. See WORLD BOOK: African Animals
2. Discover the difference between alligators and crocodiles. See: Bare, Colleen, NEVER KISS AN ALLIGATOR (Cobblehill, 1989) and Barrett, Norman, CROCODILES AND ALLIGATORS (Watts, 1989).
3. Learn about quicksand, where found and composition. See: DePaola, Tomie, THE QUICKSAND BOOK (Holiday, 1977). See also: Borden, Beatrice, THE WILD ANIMALS OF AFRICA, (Random, 1982).

LITERATURE

1. Introduce the author Verna Aardema. Find information about her in SOMETHING ABOUT THE AUTHOR library reference set.
2. Each of her picture books is set in a different *country* in Africa. Locate the settings of each country on a map.
   BIMWILI AND THE ZIMWI (Dial 85)
   BRINGING THE RAIN TO KAPITI PLAIN (Dial 81)
   OH, KOJO, HOW COULD YOU? (Dial 84)
   PRINCESS GORILLA AND A NEW KIND OF WATER (Dial 88)
   RABBIT MAKES A MONKEY OUT OF LION (Dial 89)
   VINGANANEE AND THE TREE TOAD (Viking, 83)
   WHAT'S SO FUNNY, KETU? (Dial 82)
   WHO'S IN RABBIT'S HOUSE? (Dial 76)
   WHY MOSQUITOES BUZZ IN PEOPLE'S EARS (Dial 85)
3. Use shared reading, guided reading, partnership reading and individualized reading.
4. Use story strips as a cooperative learning activity. Each student has a strip and the group lines up in story order. Strips need capital letters and punctuation which students add as they read their strips.

88

TO INTRODUCE THE UNIT:
THE VINGANANEE AND THE TREE TOAD by Verna Aardema
or WHO IS COMING? by Patricia McKissack

These picture books introduce African animals in their natural settings and provide excellent predictive reading experiences.

ANIMALS OF AFRICA: BIBLIOGRAPHY   Copyright © 1991 by Nancy Polette

FICTION:

Aardema, Verna. BIMWILI AND THE ZIMWI (Zanzibar) (Dial, 1985) A Swahili girl is abducted by a Zimwi and told to be the voice inside his singing drum .

BRINGING THE RAIN TO KAPITI PLAIN (Dial 1981) A cumulative tale about animals of the grasslands and the need for rain.

OH, KOJO, HOW COULD YOU! (Ashanti tale) (Dial, 1984) Each time Kojo is sent to buy something he is tricked out of his money by Ananse, until with the help of a cat he finally tricks the trickster.

PRINCESS GORILLA AND A NEW KIND OF WATER (A Mpongwe tale) (Dial 1988). King Gorilla decrees that no one may marry his daughter until a suitor strong enough to consume a barrel of strange, smelly water can be found.

VINGANANEE AND THE TREE TOAD (Liberia) (Viking, 1983). A strange animal called the Vingananee beats up all the other animals and eats their stew until tiny Tree Toad offers to fight him.

WHAT'S SO FUNNY KETU? (Nuer tale) (Dial, 1982) For saving the life of a snake, Ketu is rewarded by being allowed to hear animals think.

WHO'S IN RABBIT'S HOUSE? (Masai tale) (Dial, 1976) Rabbit has a problem . Someone is inside her house and won't let her in.

WHY MOSQUITOES BUZZ IN PEOPLE'S EARS (Dial 1985) Mosquito tells a tall tale which results in the sun not rising.

Arego, Jose. WE HIDE, YOU SEEK. (Greenwillow, 1979) African animals are hidden in their natural settings as rhino tries to find them.

Base, Graeme. ANAMALIA, (Abrams, 1986) Alliteration and illustrations that require close observation! Not all African animals.

Brown, Margaret Wise. THE IMPORTANT BOOK. (Harper Trophy Edition, 1990) A delightful pattern book that can be used to develop pattern paragraphs.

Elting, Mary. Q IS FOR DUCK, (Houghton Mifflin, 1980) Q is for Duck! Why! Because ducks quack. A pattern ABC book with a difference.

Hutchins, Pat. 1 HUNTER. (Mulberry Books, 1986). Animals are behind the hunter who is seeking them.

Seeger, Pete. ABIYOYO (Macmillan, 1988) A boy and his father save the village from the giant creature, Abiyoyo.

NON FICTION :

Stone, Colleen. NEVER KISS AN ALLIGATOR. (Cobblehill, 1989) For primary grades an easy reading introduction to alligators with color photographs.

Barrett, Norman. CROCODILES AND ALLIGATORS, (Watts,1989) Details the differences-with charts and illustrations. Higher reading level- gr. 4-6.

Borden, Beatrice. WILD ANIMALS OF AFRICA. (Random House, 1982) Picture book introduction to African animals.

dePaola, Tomie. THE QUICKSAND BOOK, (Holiday,1977) Jungle girl falls in the quicksand and receives a lecture from jungle boy all about quicksand before he pulls her out. Recipe for making quicksand included.

Georges, D.V., THE TRUE BOOK OF AFRICA. (Children's Press, 1986) Full color photographs, maps, easy vocabulary make this an excellent introduction to Africa for primary grades.

Glubok, Shirley. THE ART OF AFRICA. (Macmillan, 1974) Large picture book with spare text to introduce the art of Africa.

Simon, Seymour. ANIMAL FACT, ANIMAL FABLE. (Crown, 1979) Challenge children to find the African animals in the book! A statement about an animal is made on one page with the question, "Is it fact or fable?" The answer along with an explanation appears on the next page.

SHARED READING
WITH VERNA AARDEMA BOOKS ▣

Books by Verna Aardema which are particularly useful in shared reading experiences because of their repeating patterns are:

WHY MOSQUITOES BUZZ IN PEOPLE'S EARS (Dial, 1975)

BRINGING THE RAIN TO KAPITI PLAIN (Dial 1981)

THE VINGANANEE AND THE TREE TOAD (Warne, 1983)

The shared reading experience consists of a model reader reading aloud while others join in. In primary grades "big books", those with print large enough to be seen at a distance, are often used. Overhead transparencies also work well.

The model reader should read slowly enough so that children can follow the line of print as the reader's hand moves along the line. Model reading includes pausing at appropriate points in the text and using the rise or fall of the voice appropriately.

Shared reading materials can include the text of a story, poetry, song lyrics, chants or any other material.

Techniques for shared reading include:

REPETITION: Sharing the story or poem many times.

PATTERNING: Selecting stories or poems with repeating patterns.

ECHO READING: Reading a line from a poem and having children repeat or echo the line.

TRACKING: Moving the hand or finger along the line being read as children listen to establish the connection between what they are seeing and what they are hearing.

FADING: As children grow confident in their ability to read the text the model reader gradually softens his/her voice and stops reading while the young readers continue.

SHARED READING is equally appropriate for older students through senior high school when they meet new language patterns. Shakespeare, for example, must be read aloud and modeled before students can read with meaning.

A LETTER TO SHARE WITH YOUNG READERS FROM VERNA AARDEMA

Dear Young Reader,

Would you like to know how this bookworm hatched into a writer?

There were 11 people in my family, in the little town of New Era, Michigan. Every meal was like a family reunion. When I was about 11 years old, I used to run away to the swamp (near our house) before the meal to escape having to set the table. And after the meal, to get out of helping with the dishes.

My mother let me get away with that because she knew that I wanted to become a writer. And she thought the swamp was a good place for the metamorphosis.

It really was in a dark "secret room" of that swamp that I made up my first stories. I would sit on a log, dig my heels into the spongy black earth, and think and think until I'd think it must be safe to return to the house.

Mama set me up in business with an old gray ledger left from the days when my father had owned a store. She tore out the used pages. In the half that was left, I wrote the little stories which I thought of in the swamp, and asked God to help me to become as good a writer as Gene (Stratton) Porter - who was my favorite author at that time.

With God and my mother behind me, I couldn't fail!

Here's wishing you happy reading and successful writing!

Verna Aardema

THE VINGANANEE AND THE TREE TOAD
BY VERNA AARDEMA ▣

A strange animal who looks like a "one big bushy tail" beats up all the other animals and eats their stew. Tiny Tree Toad offers to get rid of the Vingananee. When Big Lion and Buck Deer could not fight the creature, how will Tree Toad get rid of him?

State the problem here:
In what way or ways can Tree Toad _____
_____ ?

List ideas in the boxes below after the numbers 1, 2, 3, and 4.

Score each idea by giving a 3 if the answer is **yes**, a 2 if the answer is **maybe** and a 1 of the answer is no. The first one is done for you.

SCORING: 1 = no 2 = maybe 3 = yes	Will it not hurt Tree Toad?	Can they keep the stew?	Will it be fast?	Will it work?	Total
1. Throw the stew on the Vinganansee.	2	1	2	2	7
2.					
3.					
4.					

Total the scores for each idea.

The best solution is _____ .

RECALLING THE STORY 🔟
THE VINGANANEE AND THE TREE TOAD
BY VERNA AARDEMA
Telling the Story in Song
(Sing to the tune of "Waltzing Matilda")

Here comes the (1) S _____

Here comes the (2) L _____

Here comes the (3) B _____ D _____

  friends eating stew.

Then came the (4) B_____ T _____

Beat the friends and tied them up,

Oh, my! Oh, dear! Now what can they do?

There goes the (5) S _____

There goes the (6) L _____

There goes the (7) B _____ D _____

  all went away.

Then came the (8) T _____ T _____

Fell upon the big beast's head.

Friends now awake to a brighter day.

RECALLING THE STORY 🔟

THE VINGANANEE AND THE TREE TOAD
BY VERNA AARDEMA

Directions: Cut apart the story cards and give one card to each student. The student with the starred card begins by reading the WHO HAS portion of the card. The student who can answer the question with his/her card reads the answer and then reads the WHO HAS portion of his/her card. The game continues until all cards are read.

I HAVE: Tree Toad said, "It was a miracle!". WHO HAS: What did Spider buy? *	I HAVE: The Vingananee dragged Lion behind the house and tied him up. WHO HAS: What did Spider say when the animals told her that is was her turn to fight the Vingananee?
I HAVE: Spider bought a farm. WHO HAS: What animals lived with Spider?	I HAVE: Spider said, "I am too small." WHO HAS: What did Tree Toad offer to do?
I HAVE: Lion and Buck Deer lived with Spider. WHO HAS: What strange animal tied up rat and ate the stew?	I HAVE: Tree Toad offered to fight the Vingananee. WHO HAS: What did the Vingananee do to Tree Toad?
I HAVE: The Vingananee tied up rat and ate the stew. WHO HAS: What did the Vingananee do to Buck Deer?	I HAVE: The Vingananee tossed Tree Toad up into the sky. WHO HAS: How did the Tree Toad win the fight with the Vingananee?
I HAVE: The Vingananee tied Buck Deer up behind the house. WHO HAS: What did the Vingananee do to Lion?	I HAVE: Tree Toad fell so hard on the Vingananee's head that she knocked him out. WHO HAS: What did Tree Toad say about winning the fight with the Vingananee?

94

WHO IS COMING?
by Patricia McKissack
Children's Press, 1986

FOR THE TEACHER: This is a beginning reader about a little monkey in Africa who meets and runs away from a variety of African animals. It introduces prepositions as monkey runs "up the tree", "in the water" and "under the lion." The surprise ending will teach children something about Africa that many people do not know.

Topic Talking 🔲6

1. Assign partners.
2. State a topic: monkeys.
3. Partner A talks on the topic to B until you say "Switch" (after 10 seconds).
4. Partner B talks on the same topic until you say "Stop" (10 seconds).
5. Follow the procedure with a second topic, African animals, (30 seconds) and a third topic, Africa, (one minute).
6. Over a period of time slowly increase the amount of time *and* the size of the group.

As students show progress in their ability to speak easily on a topic the groups might be increased to three or four so that one child is talking to two or three others.

Topics can be assigned in advance so that children can prepare for them or topics can be given that most children can talk easily about (for example, *Pets*.)

A variation of this procedure is to have Partner A speak on the topic to Partner B for a specified length of time. Then Partner B tells Partner A *What Partner A said*. This encourages attentive listening.

Predicting words in the story 🔲5

This is a story about a little monkey who runs away from animals who are running after him. Two of these animals are *not* in the story. Can you guess which two are *not* in the story?

alligator	hippopotamus
leopard	crocodile
lion	snake
elephant	giraffe

Listen to the story and see if your guesses were right.

Alligator and giraffe were not in the story.

WRITING SONGS ABOUT [20] "WHO IS COMING?" Grades 1-3

Writing songs to check story comprehension and to teach sentence structure

Who Is Coming?: Reviewing the story

Pattern for: Are You Sleeping?

LITTLE	BROWN	MONKEY
adjective	adjective	name of a character

LITTLE		MONKEY
adjective	adjective	name of a character

_____

prepositional phrase telling where the character was

_____

prepositional phrase telling where the character was

_____ and _____
ing verb   ing verb

_____ and _____
ing verb   ing verb

RUN AWAY
three syllable word or phrase to end the story

STAY AND PLAY
another three syllable word or phrase or repeat three syllable word or phrase above

Pattern for: Skip to My Lou

LITTLE	MONKEY	CLIMBING	UP THE TREE
adjective	noun	verb	prepositional phrase

adjective	noun	verb	prepositional phrase

adjective	noun	verb	prepositional phrase

RUN, LITTLE MONKEY, RUN, RUN!
seven syllable last line (any part of speech)

96

WHO IS COMING?

Directions: Cut the story strips apart. Give one to each child. Children line up in the order of the story. When reading the story, each child adds capital letters and periods where needed.

monkey ran from crocodile

monkey ran from snake

monkey ran from leopard

monkey ran from lion

monkey ran from elephant

monkey ran from hippo

monkey did not run from tiger why

there are no tigers in africa

ANIMAL CHARACTERISTICS
Paragraph Writing

1. Name African animals. Add six more names to this list.

2. Group the animals. Add three more groups.

	Hippo	Lion	Leopard	Elephant	Gorilla					
mammal	X									
reptile										
bird										
meat eater										
plant eater	X									
mountain animal										
jungle animal	X									
grasslands animal										
desert animal										

3. Under each animal name put an X in the boxes which describe the animal. The first animal, **Hippo**, is done for you.

4. Choose one animal. Use information from the chart above to write an "important" paragraph about the animal. Follow the example given in writing your paragraph.

The Hippo _____ [26]

animal name

The important thing about the hippo is that it is a mammal. It lives in the jungle and eats plants. But the important thing about a hippo is that it is a mammal.

The important thing about a _____ is that it _____

_____ .

It _____

and _____

but the important thing about a _____ is that it _____

_____ .

PARAGRAPH CONSTRUCTION ▨

Responding to a visual

PROCEDURE:
1. Make an overhead transparency of the visual.

2. Display the visual and ask students to list name words, describing words and action words related to the visual. Provide students with small 'postits' or slips of paper so that each word can be written on a separate piece of paper. Students can work alone or in small groups with each member of the group contributing a word in turn.

3. When students have large banks of words, ask them to select from their word banks those words which will make a sentence describing the picture. Explain that this is a topic sentence.

4. Encourage students to share their completed sentences orally.

5. Challenge students to use other words in their word banks to add one or more details about the picture in sentence form. Explain that a paragraph contains a topic sentence and other sentences that add details about the topic. Allow sufficient time for students to develop their sentences.

6. Share the story from which the visual is taken.

DESCRIBING ANIMALS

Now try this:

Think of an animal to write about. Think about the things that it does or habits it might have. What would it do?

Some _____ have their own _____

where they _____ .

Sometimes they go around

_____

or sometimes they just

_____

But to this very day, some _____

have their own _____ .

AFRICAN ANIMALS

Fun ways to report on an animal.

1. Make a True/False book like Seymour Simon's *Animal Fact, Animal Fable*. Draw a picture and write a sentence about an animal on one page. Ask your reader if the statement is true or false. On the next page draw another picture and tell whether the statement is true or false and why.

A.

FACT OR FICTION?	FICTION
Lions live in the jungle.	Lions live in the grasslands of Africa, not in the jungle.

B. Write an acrostic poem about an animal.

L ions live in Africa.
I n tall grasses.
O ne lion can move very quietly.
N anny goats are a lion's favorite meal.

C. Follow this pattern to write a "Foot" poem about an animal.

If I had the feet of a <u>rhino</u>,
I'd <u>have an odd number of toes on each foot</u>,
And I'd <u>have weak eyesight, but acute hearing and a strong sense of</u>
<u>smell</u>,
But I wouldn't <u>be very active at night</u>
Because <u>armadillos</u> do that.

Basic model:
If I had the feet of _____ ,
I'd _____
and I'd _____
but I wouldn't _____
because _____ do that.

101

PICK A PROJECT! 🖾
A Research Organizer

Step One:	**Step Two:**	**Step Three:**

Step One:
Choose and circle one action word

Label

List

Describe

Locate

Report

Show

Group

Discover

Compose

Create

Demonstrate

Choose

Tell About

Step Two:
Choose and circle one topic

Animals of Africa
I. Kinds of African wildlife
   A. Mammals
   B. Reptiles
   C. Birds

II. Where the animals live
   A. Mountain animals
   B. Jungle animals
   C. Desert animals
   D. Grassland animals

III. Researching one animal
   A. Red deer
   B. Hyena
   C. Crocodile
   D. Elephant
   E. Hippopotamus
   F. Leopard
   G. Zebra
   H. Lion
   I. Giraffe
   J. Chimpanzee
   K. Camel

Step Three:
Choose and circle one product

Acrostic poem

Chart

Story

Model

Map

Mobile

Diorama

Bio-poem

Report

True/false book

Drawing

Write a sentence telling what you will do to report on the topic you choose. In your sentence include an action word and a product as well as your topic.

_____

_____action_____topic_____product_____

_____

Integrated Literature Studies

pic: Books with a Dickensian flavour!   Grade Levels: 4-7

> Begin with: Reading of one or both short novels by Sid Fleischman: *The Whipping Boy* (1986) or *The Midnight Horse* (1990) both published by Greenwillow Books.

LITERATURE

Group vocabulary words before reading the story.

Write for five minutes daily on open ended questions for each chapter in pre-reading journals.

Sequence story action with story strips.

Compare what you learn about thieves and cutthroats in these two books with the thief in Alfred Noyes' famous poem, The Highwayman.

Compare literary elements (character, setting, plot, theme, mood, point of view) in the two books and with books by Leon Garfield and Joan Aiken.

Complete a literary book review using poetry patterns.

LANGUAGE ARTS

1. Find examples of descriptive writing in either book. Note the author's use of simile.
2. Capitalize and punctuate story strips.
3. Respond to one illustration in either story by producing many words related to the illustration and arrange words in sentence order.
4. Research a topic related to the story and report using a divergent product model (acrostic poem, true/false book, mystery person report, limmerick, write a letter report, news article, editorial, interview, TV show script).

SOCIAL STUDIES

What countries would not have been on a map in Prince Brat's schoolroom 200 years ago?

How would a sheriff 200 years ago view a police station today?

Discover whether whipping boys really existed in history.

Name some kings or queens ruling today. Describe one day in the life of one real ruler you select.

List the qualities of a good ruler. Rank order by importance.

SCIENCE

Research the problem of rats in large cities 200 years ago and today.

Long ago garlic was considered a cure for many illnesses. Is it considered a cure today? Why or why not?

If Prince Brat, Jemmy or Touch had been injured, would they have been treated with antiseptics? anesthesia?

HEALTH

1. The thieves' diet consisted of garlic, salt herring and coarse bread. Is this nutritional? What might happen if you ate only these three things?

HIGHER ORDER THINKING

uency: Name many tales with royalty.

exibility: Group the tales.

aboration: Add details to the description of one character to make that character stand out in the reader's mind.

recasting: What caused Prince Brat to run away? What were the effects on him? On others in the palace? What caused the Judge to withhold Touch's inheritance? What were the effects of this action?

nalyze one title by Fleischman, Garfield, Aiken and *Oh, Brother* by Yorinks for Dickens' elements.

FINE ARTS

Find a painting by an artist who might have painted in Jemmy's day (200 years ago).
Find a painting by an artist who might have painted during Touch's day (100 years ago).
Write a poem to accompany the painting you find.

PARAGRAPH CONSTRUCTION ▧

Responding to a visual

PROCEDURE:
1. Make an overhead transparency of the visual.

2. Display the visual and ask students to list name words, describing words and action words related to the visual. Provide students with small 'postits' or slips of paper so that each word can be written on a separate piece of paper. Students can work alone or in small groups with each member of the group contributing a word in turn.

3. When students have large banks of words, ask them to select from their word banks those words which will make a sentence describing the picture. Explain that this is a topic sentence.

4. Encourage students to share their completed sentences orally.

5. Challenge students to use other words in their word banks to add one or more details about the picture in sentence form. Explain that a paragraph contains a topic sentence and other sentences that add details about the topic. Allow sufficient time for students to develop their sentences.

6. Share the story from which the visual is taken.

Illustration by Peter Sis from *The Whipping Boy* by Sid Fleischman. Greenwillow Books, 1986. Reprinted with permission.

THE DICKENS YOU SAY! 🎞️ 18

Sid Fleischman has written two novels with Dickensian overtones! That is, many of the elements found in a Fleischman novel are also found in a novel by Charles Dickens. Recall Dickens' stories you have seen on television. Add to this list of elements usually found in a Dickens' novel.

Orphans alone in the world.	A kind or helpful benefactor	Spirits/ghosts
A cruel, uncaring person	Thieves/cutthroats	Dirty crowded cities
	Children forced to steal	

As you read one or both of these Sid Fleischman novels, note the Dickensian elements present.

THE WHIPPING BOY
1987 Newbery Medal Winner
Sid Fleischman
Greenwillow Books 1986

He is known throughout the land as Prince Brat, a name he justly deserves! In his kingdom it is forbidden to spank the heir to the throne. So an orphan named Jemmy is plucked from the streets to serve as a whipping boy.

Jemmy dreams of running away but finds himself saddled with the prince who is less than a desirable companion. Captured by cutthroats, Jemmy plans the prince's rescue which the prince refuses to accept.

Escaping from thieves, bears, rats and other dangers, the two boys survive and the lives of both are changed forever.

Compare the setting, plot and themes of these tales with the picture book, *Oh Brother* by Arthur Yorinks (Farrar 1989) Why would it, too, be called a Dickensian tale?

THE MIDNIGHT HORSE
Sid Fleischman
Greenwillow Books, 1990

It is raining bullfrogs! Inside the coach to Cricklewood sit a blacksmith, a thief, and an orphan boy named Touch.

"The haunt, lad!" shouts the blacksmith suddenly. "If you want to see a live ghost, stick your head out of the window. He's on the roof."

That is Touch's first glimpse of the ghost who can turn straw into horses and for some reason he feels no fear.

"Where did you say you are going, boy?" asked the blacksmith.

"To my only living relative, Judge Henry Wigglesworth, maybe you know him."

"Of course I do," said the blacksmith, "everyone does."

In a flash of lightning Touch caught sight of the other passenger with a face rough as moldy cheese and eyes as deep as potholes.

Somehow he knew all would not be well in Cricklewood. The sign by the road said, CRICKLEWOOD N. H. Population 217. 216 Fine Folks and One Grouch.
You can guess who the one grouch was!

GUESS AND GROUP ▣
Pre-reading activity

Here are words found in the first chapter of *The Whipping Boy* by Sid Fleischman. Working with partner or a small group, think of four headings. Put each word under one of the four headings. I you do not know a word, *guess* which heading to put it under. Read Chapter One to support or deny your guesses!

feast	oak	wigs	scalped	shrieked
clasped	cackle	furious	whipping boy	thrash
cuff	chamber	drafty	north tower	orphan
guard	Gaw!	defiant	contrite	exasperation
scowl	tower	bawl	spring	gloat

Here are words found in the first chapter of *The Midnight Horse* by Sid Fleischman. Group them under four headings you choose. Guess if you do not know in which group a word belongs. Read Chapter One to support or deny your guesses.

lurched	unlashed	cargo	blacksmith	thief
orphan	shavings	coach	lanky	ragman
castoff	Portsmouth	muffler	mummy	bestowed
confirm	compass	prey	moldy	knothole
haunt	pothole	snort	marigold	grouch

WHAT'S REALLY SCARY?

In *The Whipping Boy*, being held prisoner by cutthroats is scary, but Prince Brat finds that sloshing deeper into the darkening, cavernous, rat-infested sewers is terrifying!

In *The Midnight Horse*, Touch finds the threat of his uncle to put him in an orphan's home is scary, but that trying to leap across the banks of the river on a high-stepping stallion is terrifying

A writing pattern:

_____ is scary but _____ is terrifying!

Use the pattern to complete these sentences. Then add a sentence of your own that follows the pattern.

1. Getting a beating when you have done nothing wrong is scary but

    _____ is terrifying

2. Meeting a bear in the woods is scary but

    _____ is terrifying

3. Knowing a ghost is riding on top of the coach in which you are a passenger is scary but

    _____ is terrifying

4. Losing all of your money is scary but

    _____ is terrifying

WRITING AND FLEXIBLE THINKING
Pre-reading activities
EXCUSES!

From the list below choose any three items:

an apple core	a string	a rattlesnake
a dead rat	a tin soldier	bad shadows
a rusty key	six fire crackers	road tar
a one-eyed kitten	a brass doorknob	crazed deer
a kite	a broken window	mousetrap

The Whipping Boy
Master Peckwit, Prince Brat's tutor, was upset. The Prince could neither read nor write, and since the whipping boy, Jemmy, had to take the thrashings for the Prince's misdeeds, the Prince did not care whether he had his lessons or not. Everyday the Prince has a new excuse for not showing up with his homework. Write an excuse for today, using three of the items in the list above.

_____

_____

_____

_____

_____

In *The Midnight Horse*, the orphan, Touch, goes to his Uncle to claim the inheritance left him by his father who was lost at sea. A great deal of money had been left the boy but the uncle claims that there is only thirty-seven cents left. Write an excuse that the uncle gives to Touch to explain why there is no money left. Include at least three of the items above in the excuse.

_____

_____

_____

_____

_____

PREDICTING ACTION IN A STORY
Pre-reading activity

In the story of *The Whipping Boy*, Prince Brat refuses to learn to read or write. The outlaws insist that he send a note to his father, the king, demanding ransom.

Suppose that Prince Brat simply wanted his father to know he is safe and also wants to tell his father of his travels. He might purchase a ready-made letter like the one below; have someone read it to him and check the boxes that will best tell of his adventures.

BEFORE READING THE STORY, check the boxes you think Prince Brat might choose.

Dear Father:
1. I ran away to:
    a. __ avoid a whipping
    b. __ relieve boredom
    c. __ join the circus

2. I was captured by:
    a. __ a smelly robber
    b. __ a two headed dragon
    c. __ a girl with a pet bear

3. I escaped by:
    a. __ becoming invisible
    b. __ changing myself into a cat
    c. __ running away

4. I was surprised to learn that the people of our kingdom:
    a. __ want a new king
    b. __ thought that the whipping boy had kidnapped me
    c. __ call me Prince Brat

5. To escape further danger I hid in:
    a. __ an underground cave
    b. __ a sewer full of rats
    c. __ an apple barrel

6. During my travels I learned a lot about:
    a. __ rats and rat fights
    b. __ trusting others
    c. __ myself

Answers: 1.B 2.A 3.C 4.C 5.B 6.C

PRE-READING JOURNAL

Here are open ended sentence beginnings for each chapter of *The Whipping Boy* by Sid Fleischman. **Before reading**, select one or more of the sentence starters and:

Report orally to a partner on the topic for two minutes,

or

Write for five minutes on the sentence starter you choose. Pre-reading journals are not collected but you will be asked to read what you have written to a partner or group.

Chapter

1	When one person is punished for the misdeeds of another.......
2	A broken promise can lead to.........
3	Running away from home.........
4	Walking through a fog-filled forest.........
5	Cutthroats intend to..........
6	Ransom means...........
7	A person who doesn't know when to keep quiet.......
8	A wagon load of gold can be traded for...........
9	Not knowing how to read can be dangerous when.........
10	The outlaw was so skinny that ....
11	Cutting off your nose to spite your face means........
12	Tricking outlaws (is, isn't) wrong because ....
13	Chasing a bear can be ....
14	The problems with being a Prince are..........
15	Abandoning a friend in time of need.........
16	Betrayal means ....
17	A bear riding in a coach.................
18	"Clothes make the man" means..................
19	Leaping before one looks can lead to ....
20	Trust means..............

THE WHIPPING BOY: STORY STRIPS ▣

Cut apart, give one strip to each student . Students line up in the order in which the events occurred. Once the order is correct, each student should indicate the missing capital letters and punctuation marks in his or her strip.

prince brat laughs as jemmy is punished for the princes

misdeeds   jemmy runs away and the prince goes with him

the prince and jemmy are captured by cutthroats and

held prisoner the prince refuses to deliver the ransom note

the boys escape but the prince refuses to go home

the prince takes a beating from the scoundrels without

crying in the city he enjoys shaking hands

can i help share the work he asks

jemmy and the prince are chased through the sewers by

the cutthroats the boys escape and the prince takes jemmy

back to the palace for a reward

the prince vows to become a good king to his people by

accepting responsibility

Look again! For each of the events above, which is caused by someone being irresponsible and by someone being responsible?

BOOK REPORTS 🏁

he poetry patterns on this page are all used to describe a character or scene from 'he Whipping Boy or *The Midnight Horse*. Choose a scene or character from this or nother favorite tale and use one of the patterns below to tell about it.

Five Senses Poem
(The Whipping Boy)

olor	The sewer was black as night
ound	It sounded like shrill chatterings
aste	It tasted like yesterday's garbage.
mell	It smelled like the nest of a rat.
ight	It looked like midnight with no moon.
eeling	It made Prince Brat feel like fleeing.

Phone Number Poem
(The Whipping Boy)

ach line has the number of syllables in chosen phone number.

Two young boys
Ran away
Caught by cutthroats
Prince Brat refused to be freed
Jemmy ran away
Prince Brat ran after him
Hardship changed his outlook

Adverb Poem
(The Midnight Horse)

Adverb	Strongly
Adverb	Firmly
Adverb	Emphatically
Noun	The Judge
Verb	Refused
Noun with description	The poor boy's
Any word	Inheritance

Build A Name Poem

J
U
D
G
E

W
I
G
G
L
E
S
W
O
R
T
H

Bio Poem
(The Midnight Horse)

Line		
1	First name	Touch
2	Four traits	
3	Related to	
4	Cares deeply about	
5	Who feels	
6	Who needs	
7	Who gives	
8	Who fears	
9	Who would like to see	
10	Resident of	

CHOOSING A READING RESPONSE PROJECT FOR THE MIDNIGHT HORSE and THE WHIPPING BOY

1. Select one of the topics listed below. Each topic is related in some way to the story of *The Whipping Boy* or *The Midnight Horse* by Sid Fleischman.
2. Select an action word.
3. Select a product. Write a project statement like the examples below.

ACTION (Choose one)	TOPIC (Choose one)	PRODUCT (Choose one)
Knowledge Define Record Label List **Comprehension** Summarize Describe Locate Report **Application** Solve Demonstrate Dramatize Show **Analysis** Compare Categorize Classify Discover **Synthesis** Compose Hypothesize Predict Create **Evaluation** Judge Rank order Criticize Recommend	Literary Topics The character of Jemmy The character of Touch The setting of *The Whipping Boy* and the setting of *The Midnight Horse* Use of similes in either story The theme of responsibility in either story Other books about orphans The thieves in either story compared to "The Highwayman" by Alfred Noyes or those in *Smith* by Leon Garfield. Non-fiction Topics The practice of having a whipping boy at the royal palace Travel before the automobile Rat fighting Qualities of a good ruler ... outstanding kings or queens in history The fate of orphans 100 or more years ago Famous orphans: Charles Dickens, Edgar Allen Poe, Jack London, others? Kings or queens ruling today ... a day in the life of ... More titles with a Dickensian flavour Aiken, Joan. *Black Hearts in Battersea*. Doubleday 1964. *Wolves of Willoughby Chase*. Doubleday 1963. Garfield, Leon. *Fair's Fair*. Doubleday, 1983. *Jack Holborn*. Pantheon, 1965. *Smith*, Pantheon, 1967.	Acrostic poem Advice letter Autobiography Bio-poem Chart Choral reading Collage Comic strip Concert reading Diorama Editorial Essay Eyewitness report Fable Filmstrip Interview Journal Lesson Map Model Moment in history script Mystery person report Newspaper Oral report Poem Question/answer session Readers theatre script Report Song Story Tape recording Time line TV script True/false book

EXAMPLES

ACTION	TOPIC	PRODUCT
Describe	the character of Jemmy	as an acrostic poem
Criticize	the practice of having a whipping boy	in an editorial

INTEGRATING WHOLE LANGUAGE COMPONENTS IN THE READING PROGRAM: middle school/junior high

Children who move from a whole language program in the primary grades have many characteristics in common:

1. Many like to read and spend time in self-selected reading.
2. They like to write and have had success as authors who write for a specific audience and have seen their work "published" as class books.
3. They are collaborative learners, working together and helping each other.
4. They are used to making choices in their learning activities.
5. They often bring their own experience to the learning activity.

Each of the above characteristics translates into basic components of a whole language program and can become a part of middle school /junior high school reading programs in the following ways:

. Rather than every child being given the same story for study, literature should be organized by themes and a wide variety of fiction and non-fiction available on the theme from which students can choose both their reading and their projects.

. Partnership reading with each child reading a book on his or her level should be encouraged. For a description of partnership reading see page 42.

. Reading discussion groups and reading conferences are encouraged. Discussion groups can compare and contrast the variety of books read on the same theme. A short teacher/student reading conference allows the teacher to hear the student read aloud self-selected passages, retell a part of the story in his/her own words, answer questions relating the story to the overall theme and make plans for additional reading and reading response products.

. The middle school/junior high school version of the shared book experience can be done with the reading together of poetry; choral reading; or reading together short prose passages with appropriate student-selected background music to set the mood.

. Writing in response to literature and using authors' works as models for students' own creative writing is encouraged. Work should always have a purpose and students must be provided with an audience for their writing through publication in class anthologies or as individual books.

. Author studies are very appropriate for middle school/junior high school students as are oral book talks on favorite novels done to self selected music to set the mood.

. Fluent and flexible thinking should be encouraged to stretch students beyond the one right answer mode of thinking. In addition, whenever possible, pull from students' experiences and allow choice in reading material and response products.

Integrated Literature Studies

Topic: Ocean Voyages   Grade Levels: 5-9

Begin with: Introduce with a book talk: *The True Confessions of Charlotte Doyle* by Avi. Orchard Books, 1990.

LITERATURE

Responding to literature: Book reports: As songs, acrostic poems, interviews with a main character (see product list page 123).

Kipling: *How The Whale Got Its Throat* (Use as a model for writing your own "how" tale having to do with the ocean)

Stevenson: *Treasure Island* (Perform a scene as a concert reading)

Verne: *20,000 Leagues Under The Sea* (Appear as Capt. Neemo to answer questions from the class)

Longfellow: "Wreck of the Hesperus" (Use as a model for writing a poem about another historical sea disaster)

LANGUAGE ARTS

Form flexible literature response groups for oral discussion of novels on ocean travel. Use question starters for discussion like "How many ways", "What if", "If you were..", "How is _____ like _____ ."

Compare fictional and actual accounts of legendary pirates (ex: Jean Laffite). Report on the differences.

Write an original poem based on a factual account of a real sea voyage.

Write a book talk to present with background music for a novel you have read about a sea voyage.

SOCIAL STUDIES

Read Lord's *Night To Remember*. Write and perform a "To Test the Truth" TV script where three students pretend to be a passenger. Students guess who the real passenger or eyewitness was.

Read an account of a famous ocean voyage (ex: The Mayflower). Compare the account with a literary account (Ex: Heman's poem "The Landing of the Pilgrim Fathers" compare the two for accuracy. Compare voyages of two explorers: Ex: Sir Francis Drake and Prince Henry.

SCIENCE

Read Verne's *20,000 Leagues Under The Sea* (Written in 1870). Identify those fantasy elements in the book that are real today.

Read books by Jacques Cousteau and Rachel Carson. Write an eyewitness report of one of their scientific expeditions or findings about the ocean.

MATH

Provision a ship with a crew of ten for a sailing ship voyage from England to North America in 1832. Calculate time, amount of food needed daily, water needs etc.

Compare 1832 time with travel time today.

GETTING STARTED

1. Visit the school library, collect as many books (on many different reading levels) on ocean voyages as possible.

2. Assign a group of students to browse the books and group by type of voyage.

3. Brainstorm with the class all types of ocean voyages. What other books do we need?

4. Introduce as many of the books as possible. Students choose those they want to read and respond to.

FINE ARTS

Find paintings about the sea. Find a poem that is compatible with each painting. Show the painting and read the poem. Play symphonic music about the ocean in the background.

A VOYAGE OF COURAGE!

The True Confessions of Charlotte Doyle by Avi. Orchard Books, 1990.

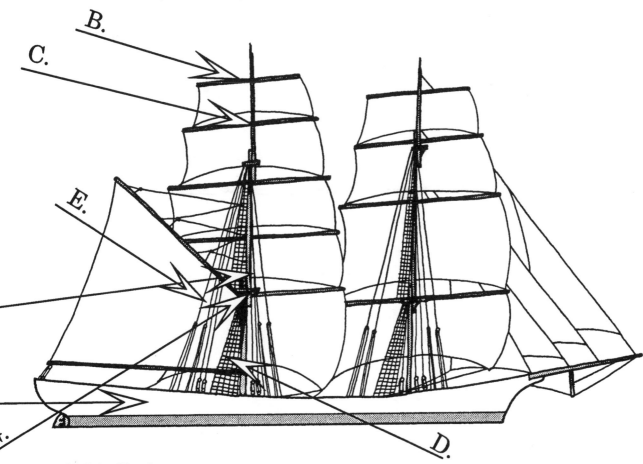

1. Royal Main Yard
2. Topsail Spar
3. Stays
4. Main Yard
5. Trestletree
6. Ratlines
7. Deck

Here is an exciting tale of a young girl caught up in the dangerous, unpredictable world of a sailing ship. At one point in the story (chapter thirteen) she must climb from the deck to the top of the highest sail of the ship. Before reading or hearing this chapter read aloud, guess the position on the ship of each part listed above. Put the number of each where you think it belongs. You might want to prepare a book talk about this dangerous climb and share it with the class. Give classmates this drawing so that they can follow every inch of her assent.

A Pre-Reading Activity: Topic Talking

1. Assign partners. Partner A talks to partner B for fifteen seconds on the topic of OCEAN VOYAGES. The teacher says "switch" and partner B talks on the same topic to partner A for fifteen seconds.

2. State the second topic (SAILING SHIPS). Talking time for each partner is 30 seconds.

3. State the third topic (DANGERS AT SEA). Each student talks for 45 seconds. To vary the procedure, partner B can tell partner A what A said.

Answers: (A) Deck, (B) Royal Main Yard, (C) Topsail Spar, (D) Ratlines, (E) Stays, (F) Main Yard, (G) Trestletree

OPEN ENDED SENTENCES
FOR THE PRE-READING JOURNAL

Students select one open-ended sentence to respond to for about five minutes in their pre-readin
journals. Journals are not collected or graded by the teacher. However, students are expected to
read aloud what they have written either to members of a small group or to the class.

The True Confessions of Charlotte Doyle by Avi. Orchard Books, 1990

Chapters One to Five

1. An ocean voyage on a sailing ship from England to the United States in 1832 would be...........

2. When sailors refuse at any price to sign on a ship with one particular captain...........

3. To a well brought up young lady of thirteen on her first voyage, rough sailors might appear to be.........

4. The way to tell a liar from one who is truthful is...........

5. Mutiny means............

Chapters Six to Ten

6. One way to tell a true friend from a scoundrel is.......

7. Reporting the grumblings of a ship's crew to the captain can lead to.......

8. Ignorance is no excuse means.............

9. When one's actions cause great harm to others even though not intended.........

Chapters Eleven to Fifteen

10. Restitution means...........

11. The most dangerous job on a sailing ship would be........

12. Making an enemy of a villainous captain can lead to...........

13. A sailing ship in a hurricane...........

Chapters Sixteen to Twenty-Two

14. People who know right from wrong sometimes do not speak out at injustice because.........

15. Choosing the easy way out of a difficult situation.........

16. After being a member of a ship's crew, the life of a New England young lady would be.........

17. In this novel, Avi is saying ....

RESPONDING TO LITERATURE
Middle School/Junior High
AN ABC PROFILE OF A NOVEL

Create an ABC profile of a novel using every letter of the alphabet at least once.

For each letter of the alphabet, think of someone or something from the novel that illustrates that letter. Be sure to explain why/how the person, place or thing you have used to illustrate your letter relates to the plot, theme, and/or character motivation/development in the novel.

NOVEL: *The True Confessions of Charlotte Doyle* **by Avi. Orchard, 1990**

is for adventure. Charlotte sets out on a sea voyage home thinking she will be looked after by another family. When she discovers she is the only passenger she is apprehensive. The ADVENTURE begins when she receives a dagger from the old cook for protection.

is for BEWARE. There are warnings all around Charlotte which she chooses not to heed until it is too late!

is for CHARLOTTE Doyle, the main character in the story who starts the voyage as a pampered young lady and ends it as a seasoned member of the crew.

Responding using the model found in Margaret Wise Brown's *Important Book*
Harper Trophy 1990

Using this pattern the student makes a statement about the novel read, adds details, then summarizes using the opening statement. This example is a book report for Walter Lord's *A Night to Remember*.

A Night to Remember by Walter Lord

The important thing about the Titanic was that it sank. It sailed in 1912 from England with over 2200 people aboard. It was boarded by many wealthy people including Molly Brown. On the night of April 14 it hit an iceberg. Only 700 people lived to say that the most important thing about the Titanic was that it sank.

WHAT CAN YOU DO WITH A POEM?

1. Read aloud with background music.
2. Read aloud with rhythm music.
3. Sing it!
4. Elaborate! Add actions or sound effects.
5. Use as a writing model.
6. Pick out key words in each line and write a mini poem.
7. Learn about the poet or research the story behind the poem.
8. For illustrated poems, read without showing the illustrations. Let students visualize. Compare their mind pictures with the artist's illustrations.
9. Integrate with content areas.
10. Do echo reading.

POEMS ABOUT MEMORABLE VOYAGES

THE WRECK OF THE HESPERUS
Henry Wadsworth Longfellow
(excerpts)

It was the schooner Hesperus
That sailed the wintry sea,
And the skipper had taken his little daughter,
To bear him company.

Down came a storm and smote amain
The vessel in its strength
She shuddered and paused like a frightened
    steed,
Then leaped her cable's length.

He wrapped his child in a seaman's coat,
Against the stinging blast;
He cut a rope from a broken spar
And bound her to the mast.

At daybreak on the bleak sea beach,
A fisherman stood aghast,
To see the form of a maiden fair
Lashed close to the drifting mast.

Mini Version

Hesperus sailed
Wintry sea,
Skipper's daughter company.
Storm smote amain
Vessel's strength
Steed leaped cable's length.

THE LANDING OF THE PILGRIM FATHERS
by Felicia Hemans

(While this poem catches the spirit of the voyage
it is filled with inaccuracies. Can you find them?

The breaking of the waves dashed high
On a stern and rockbound coast,
And the woods against a stormy sky,
Their giant branches tossed.
And the heavy night hung dark,
And the hills and water o'er,
When a band of exiles moored their bark,
On that storm-torn Plymouth shore.

The ocean eagle soared
From his nest by the white wave's foam,
And the rocking pines of the forest roared,
This was their welcome home.

About the poet:
Felicia Hemans was a housewife living in Wales.
She read a news account of a celebration
commemorating the landing of the Pilgrims. Her
poem reveals that she knew nothing of the New
World or of the actual voyage.

A FANTASY VOYAGE: READERS THEATRE

Here is a short readers theatre version of the opening event in Jules Verne's *20,000 Leagues Under the Sea*. Choose parts and perform it for the class. Use the script as a model for writing another readers theatre script based on an incident in this book or in another novel about an ocean voyage.

TWENTY THOUSAND LEAGUES UNDER THE SEA

Reading Parts: (1) Mr. Aronnax   (2) Ned   (3) Narrator   (4) Captain

Mr. Aronnax: Seated on the ship's deck, Ned Land and I were chatting about one thing and another and naturally the conversation turned to the creature I had come to find, the giant unicorn. Ned, is it possible you are not convinced that the creature we are following actually exists? Have you a particular reason for doubting?

Ned: Perhaps I have, Mr. Aronnax.

Mr. Aronnax: But Ned, you, a whaler by profession, ought to be the last to doubt.

Ned: That's just it, Professor. As a whaler I have followed many a creature and harpooned a great number but I've never seen one who could scratch the plates of a steamer like this thing you're looking for is supposed to be able to do.

Mr. Aronnax: But Ned, they tell of ships which the teeth of this creature has pierced through and through. It must be a creature with a horn of great penetrating power.

Ned: Well, I've never seen it done! Hey, what's that on the port quarter?

Narrator: There, a mile and a half from the frigate a long blackish body emerged about three feet above the waves. Its tail churned violently. Every eye was turned toward it.

Ned: Captain, Sir, strange object off the port quarter.

Captain: Is the pressure up?

Ned: Yes, Sir!

Captain: Well, stoke your fires and full steam ahead.

Narrator: The creature was pursued for three quarters of an hour, but no headway was made in catching up with it.

A FANTASY VOYAGE: READERS THEATRE
(continued)

Captain: Engineer, more pressure! That animal goes quicker than any I've ever seen. Very well, let's see if it will escape our bullets. Ned, to the forecastle. Fire at will.

Mr. Aronnax: You've hit it, Ned. But wait, your bullet, it didn't penetrate. The creature's still moving.

Narrator: And move it did, as far out of reach of the whalers as it could get, until it was lost in the distance. The chase abandoned, the whalers put away harpoons and went back to normal duties aboard ship. The chase had taken most of the afternoon and dusk fell early.

Mr. Aronnax: Ned, what's that? Looks like a light.

Ned: About three miles to windward it is. Well, I've never heard of a sea creature that big giving off a light, but I'm ready to believe anything after this afternoon.

Narrator: The Captain was called and under his orders the ship coasted silently in order not to alert its adversary. It stopped about two cables length from the animal. No one breathed. Suddenly Ned's arm straightened and the harpoon was thrown. There was a sound as if the weapon had stuck a hard body. The light went out and two enormous waterspouts broke over the bridge of the whaler sweeping Mr. Arronax from the deck.

Ned: Look out! Grab him quick.

Captain: It's too late. Mr. Aronnax has found his creature, but I fear, too, that the creature has found him as well.

Narrator: The Captain was both right and wrong. Mr. Aronnax did indeed find the creature and it was a find that was to change both of their lives. Read *Twenty Thousand Leagues Under the Sea.*

The End

CONCERT READING
AND OTHER WAYS TO SHARE LITERATURE

Here is a short excerpt from Robert Louis Stevenson's *Treasure Island*. Select appropriate background music to fit the mood of the piece. Read it aloud with the background music.

THE HUNT FOR TREASURE

The party spread itself abroad, in a fan shape, shouting and leaping to and fro. About the center, and a good way behind the rest, Silver and I followed—I tethered by my rope, he ploughing, with deep pants, among the sliding gravel. From time to time, indeed, I had to lend him a hand, or he must have missed his footing and fallen backward down the hill.

We had thus proceeded for about half a mile and were approaching the brow of the plateau when the man upon the farthest left began to cry aloud, as if in terror. Shout after shout came from him, and the others began to run in his direction.

"He can't 'a found the treasure," said Old Morgan, hurrying past us from the right, "for that's clean a-top."

Indeed, as we found when we also reached the spot, it was something very different. At the foot of a pretty big pine and involved in a green creeper, which had even partly lifted some of the smaller bones, a human skeleton lay, with a few shreds of clothing, on the ground. I believe a chill struck for a moment to every heart.

Indeed, on a second glance, it seemed impossible to fancy that the body was in a natural position. But for some disarray (the work, perhaps, of the birds that had fed upon him or of the slow-growing creeper that had gradually enveloped his remains) the man lay perfectly straight—his feet pointing in one direction, his hands, raised above his head like a diver's, pointing directly in the opposite.

OTHER WAYS TO SHARE LITERATURE

- Write a true/false book about a character. Make a statement on one page and support or deny it with evidence on the next.
- Summarize the story as a poem or song. "My Bonnie Lies Over the Ocean" is a good tune for summarizing.
- Write an "I Have, Who Has?" game for the story.
- Prepare story strips for one important scene. Challenge the class to put them together correctly and add correct capitalization and punctuation.
- Come to class as a character and answer questions about your part in the story.
- Write an acrostic poem about a story character.
- Write a sequel to the story using the same characters in a new situation. Use the storyboard and incident cards to think through the story before you write.
- Select one favorite paragraph to read aloud to music.
- Prepare an "Eyewitness" report in which three people claim to be the eyewitness to an important event in the story. Only one is telling the truth. The class votes on who the real eyewitness is.

TOPIC: OCEAN VOYAGES 🔲28

1. Brainstorm as many kinds of ocean voyages as possible. Examples: Cruises, voyages fo[r] scientific data, voyages to recover artifacts from ships that have sunk, voyages of exploration, fantasy voyages, voyages told in poetry.
2. Name and group as many words as possible having to do with ocean voyages. Select fro[m] the above words or groupings those topics the class might want to know more about.

ACTION (Choose one)	TOPIC (Choose one)	PRODUCT (Choose one)

Knowledge
  Define
  Record
  Label
  List
 	
Comprehension
  Summarize
  Describe
  Locate
  Report
 	
Application
  Solve
  Demonstrate
  Dramatize
  Show
 	
Analysis
  Compare
  Categorize
  Classify
  Discover
 	
Synthesis
  Compose
  Hypothesize
  Predict
  Create
 	
Evaluation
  Judge
  Rank order
  Criticize
  Recommend
	I. Voyages of Exploration
	  A. Early explorers
	  B. Modern day explorers
	
	II. Voyages Commemorated as Poems
	  A. Wreck of the Hesperus
	  B. Landing of the Pilgrim Fathers
	    1. Information about the poet
	    2. Information about the voyage
	
	III. Fantasy Voyages in Literature
	  A. Wreck of the Zephyr: Van Allsburg
	  B. 20,000 Leagues Under the Sea: Verne
	  C. How the Whale Got His Throat: Kipling
	
	IV. Voyages Ending in Disaster
	  A. The Titanic: See A Night to Remember by Walter Lord
	  B. Wreck of the Isis: See The Lost Wreck of the Isis by R. Ballard
	  C. Sunken Treasures by Gail Gibbons
	
	V. Pirate Voyages
	  A. Jean Lafitte by Ariane Dewey
	  B. Treasure Island by R. L. Stevenson
	
	VI. Other Voyages _____
	  A. _____
	  B. _____
		Acrostic poem
		Advice letter
		Autobiography
		Bio-poem
		Chart
		Choral reading
		Collage
		Comic strip
		Concert reading
		Diorama
		Editorial
		Essay
		Eyewitness report
		Fable
		Filmstrip
		Interview
		Journal
		Lesson
		Map
		Model
		Moment in history scrip[t]
		Mystery person report
		Newspaper
		Oral report
		Poem
		Question/answer session
		Readers theatre script
		Report
		Song
		Story
		Tape recording
		Time line
		TV script
		True/false book

EXAMPLES

ACTION	TOPIC	PRODUCT
Describe	the real pirate, Jean Lafitte	as an acrostic poem
Compose	a book report on Treasure Island	as a song
Criticize	the handling of the Titanic disaster	in an editorial

OCEAN VOYAGES

bibliography to begin on:

VOYAGES OF DISCOVERY
Grosse, Jacques. *Great Voyages of Discovery*. Facts on File, 1985. RL 10
Fisher, Leonard. *Prince Henry the Navigator*. MacMillan, 1990. RL 4
Gerrard, Roy. *Sir Francis Drake*. MacMillan, 1988. RL 3

VOYAGES OF DISASTER
Callahan, Steve. *Adrift*. Houghton, 1986. RL 9
Fine, John. *Sunken Ships and Treasure*. Atheneum, 1986. RL 8
Gibbons, Gail. *Sunken Treasure*. Harper Trophy, 1988. RL 3
Lord, Walter. *A Night To Remember*. Morrow, 1990. RL 8
Lord, Walter. *The Night Lives On*. Morrow, 1986. RL 8

FANTASY VOYAGES
Kipling, Rudyard. *How The Whale Got Its Throat*. Various editions. RL 6
Verne, Jules. *20,000 Leagues Under The Sea*. (1870) Various editions. RL 8

PIRATE VOYAGES
Dewey, Arianne. *Jean Laffite*. Greenwillow, 1989. RL 3
Gorman, Carol. *T.J. and the Pirate Who Wouldn't Go Home*. Scholastic, 1990. RL 4
Sherry, Frank. *Raiders and Rebels: The Golden Age of Piracy*. Hearst, 1986. RL 9
Stevenson, Robert L. *Treasure Island*. Various editions. RL 8

VOYAGES TO THE NEW WORLD
Avi. *The True Confessions of Charlotte Doyle*. Orchard, 1990. RL 6
Jacobs, William. *Ellis Island*. Scribner, 1990. RL 4

VOYAGES IN NOVELS
Paulsen, Gary. *The Voyage of the Frog*. Orchard, 1989. RL 6

VOYAGES IN PICTURE BOOKS
Gorel, Edward. *The Zillionaire's Daughter*. Warner, 1990 RL 3
Van Allsburg, Chris. *The Wreck of the Zephyr*. Houghton, 1983 RL 3

VOYAGES COMMEMORATED BY POETS (find in collections of the poets' works)
Hemans, Felicia. *The Landing of the Pilgrim Fathers*.
Holmes, Oliver W. *Old Ironsides*.
Longfellow, Henry W. *The Wreck of the Hesperus*.
Parker, Nancy W. *The Voyage of Ludgate Hill: Travels with Robert L. Stevenson*. Harcourt, 1987.
  RL 5

Note: For every title listed here there are dozens of books equally good. As students brainstorm types of voyages the list can grow. For example: Scientific Voyages would sure call for books by Jacques Cousteau and Rachel Carson; South Sea Voyages would call for the Newbery winner, *Call It Courage*. The list can grow and grow, adding more and more favorites.

ABIYOYO by P. Seeger. Macmillan,1988. pp88-89.
ADRIFT by S. Callahan. Houghton, 1986. p123.
AKIMBA AND THE MAGIC COW by M. Miles. Four Winds, 1976. pp13,15.
ANAMALIA by G. Base. Abrams, 1986. pp88-89.
ANIMAL FACT, ANIMAL FICTION by S. Simon. Crown, 1979. pp88-89.
ART OF AFRICA by S. Glubok. Macmillan, 1974. 88-89.
BERTIE AND THE BEAR by P. Allen. Coward, 1985. p38.
BIMWILI AND THE ZIMWI by V. Aardema. Dial, 1985. 88-89.
BLACK HEARTS AT BATTERSEA by J. Aiken. Doubleday, 1964. p112.
BREED TO COME by A. Norton. Viking, 1972. 12, 14.
BROWN BEAR, BROWN BEAR by B. Martin Jr. Holt, 1983. p38.
CAKE THAT MACK ATE by R. Robart. Little, 1988. p38.
CHILDREN OF GREEN KNOWE by L.M. Boston. Harcourt, 1955. p12, 14.
CHOCOLATE TOUCH by P. S. Cating. Morrow, 1979. p13,15.
CLOCKS AND HOW THEY GO by G. Gibbons. Crowell, 1979. p13,15.
CLOUDY WITH A CHANCE OF MEATBALLS by J. Barrett. Atheneum, 1978. p13,15.
CROCODILES AND ALLIGATORS by N. Barrett. Watts, 1989. 88-89.
DANIEL BOONE: FRONTIER ADVENTURES by K. Brandt. Troll, 1983. p46.
DAUGHTER OF THE EARTH by G. McDermott. Delacourte, 1984. p12,14.
DAWN by U. Shulevitz. Farrar, 1974. p13,15.
DUSK TO DAWN by H. Hill. Crowell, 1981. p13,15.
EINSTEIN ANDERSON SHOCKS HIS FRIENDS by S. Simon. Viking, 1980. p13,15
ELLIS ISLAND by W. Jacobs. Scribner, 1990. p123
ENCYCLOPEDIA BROWN CARRIES ON by D. Sobol. Four Winds, 1980. p13,15.
FAIR'S FAIR by L. Garfield. Doubleday, 1983. p112.
FOG DRIFT MORNING by D. K. Ray. Harper, 1983. p13,15.
FOG MAGIC by J. Sauer. Viking, 1943. p12,14.
FROM THE MIXED UP FILES OF MRS BASIL E. FRANKWEILER by E. L. Konigsburg. Atheneum, 1967 p13,15.
GHOSTS OF WAR by D. Cohen. Putnam, 1990. p21.
GIRL CALLED BOY by B. Hurmence. Clarion, 1982. p12,14.
GOOD QUEEN BESS by D. Stanley. Four Winds, 1990. p76.
GRANDFATHER TWILIGHT by B. Berger. Philomel, 1984. p13, 15.
GREAT VOYAGES OF DISCOVERY by J. Broose.Facts on File,1985. p123.
GREEN BOOK by J. P. Walsh. Farrar 1982. p12,14.
GREEN FUTURES OF TYCHO by W. Sleator. Dutton,1981. p12,14.
HATTIE AND THE FOX by M. Fox. Bradbury,1986. p38.
HILDILID'S NIGHT by C. D. Ryan. Macmillan, 1986. p13,15.
HOUSE FROM MORNING TO NIGHT by D. Bour. Kane, 1985. p13,15.
HOUSE IS A HOUSE FOR ME by M. Hoberman, Viking, 1978. p13,15.
HOUSE OF DIES DREAR by V. Hamilton. Macmillan 1968. p13,15.
HOW THE WHALE GOT ITS THROAT by R. Kipling. p114,123.
HOW TO EAT FRIED WORMS by T. Rockwell. Watts, 1973. p13,15.
I HAD A CAT by M. Reeves Macmillan 1989. p30.
IDEAS OF EINSTEIN by D. E. Fisher. Holt, 1980. p13, 15.
IMPORTANT BOOK by M .W. Brown. Harper, 1990. pp88-89.
INTO THE UNKNOWN by S. Mooser. Lippincott, 1980. p13,15.
ISLAND BOY by B. Cooney. Viking, 1988. p12,14.
IT'S ALL RELATIVE. by N. H. Apfel. Lothrop, 1981. p13,15.
JACK HOLBORN by L. Garfield. Pantheon, 1965. p112.
JEAN LAFFITE by A. Dewey. Greenwillow, 1988. p24.
JEREMY VISICK by D. Wiseman. Houghton, 1981. p12,14.
LEGENDS OF THE SUN AND MOON by E. Hadley. Cambridge, 1983. p13,15.
LIFE THROUGH THE AGES by G. Caselli. Grossett, 1987. p12,14.
LITTLE HOUSE by V. L. Burton. Houghton, 1942. p12,14.
LITTLE OLD WOMAN AND THE HUNGRY CAT by N. Polette. Greenwillow, 1989. p38.
LLAMA AND THE GREAT FLOOD by E. Alexander. Harper, 1989. p65.
LOST LANDS AND FORGOTTEN PEOPLE by J. Cornell. Sterling, 1978. p13,15.
MAGIC PORRIDGE POT by P. Galdone. Clarion, 1976. p13,15.
MIDNIGHT HORSE by S. Fleischman. Greenwillow, 1990. p105-112.
MISS RUMPHIS by B. Cooney. Viking, 1982. p12,14.
MORNING, NOON AND NIGHTTIME, TOO by L. D. Hopkins. Harper, 1980. p13,15.
MS. GLEE WAS WAITING by D. Hill. Atheneum, 1978. p13, 15.
MY BACKYARD HISTORY BOOK by D. Weitzman Little Brown, 1975. p13, 15.
MY FAVORITE TIME OF YEAR by S. Pearson. Harper, 1988. p13,15.
MYSTERIES OF NATURE by R. Caras. Harcourt, 1979. p13,15.
NEW PROVIDENCE by R. von Tscharner. Harcourt, 1987. p12,14.